The Dada Veda Songbook

Copyright © 2025 by Dada Veda and RAWA Music

All rights reserved under International and Pan-American Copyright Conventions. Published in the United States by InnerWorld Publications, PO Box 1613, San Germán, Puerto Rico, 00683.

Cover Art © Michael McClure (Sudhiira)

No part of this book may be reproduced or transmitted in any form or by any means, electronic or mechanical, including photocopying, recording, or by any information storage or retrieval system, without permission in writing from the publisher, except for the inclusion of brief quotations in a review.

ISBN: 9781881717959

How to Use this Book

I started writing songs in the year 2002. I was trying to make a CD that I could sell to raise money for a kindergarten that I was running in Albania. It was a charitable project in need of funds, and I expected that this would only be a one-time endeavor. However, I continued to write songs and release albums over the years. Recently someone asked me for the lyrics and tune to one of my songs because she wanted to perform it in her live streams. I think that there may be other people who could use some of the songs that I have written to enhance their performances and even recordings. In addition, my songs are simple and beginning musicians can easily use this book to practice and build their repertoire.

My songs fall into two major categories: some of them are spiritually oriented and some of them deal with issues of social consciousness. In all the songs I have striven to provide simple lyrics there are easy to understand. Similarly, the music of the songs is equally simple and that is because I do not claim to be a virtuoso musician. Most of my songs use three or four chords and these are the basic chords the "one," the "four" and the "five" as people who are a little versed in musical theory will know. But that musical simplicity will make it easy for anyone to learn these songs. In the book below you will find chord markings indicating how to play each song and I also provide links to a place where you can listen to the melodies and the entire song. The chords that are listed are basically the ones that I recorded with. However, you can transpose them to suit your vocal needs.

In most of the songs I have given chords for the first verse, and if there are no changes in the melody you can use these chords for the rest of the song. In cases where there is a change of melody (in bridge or outro sections) then the new chords are listed.

The songs are listed in an album-by-album basis.

In addition to the songs which I have written and recorded, you will also find a section with chord charts to nine mantra chanting (kirtan) tutorials which I posted to YouTube. The links to the video tutorials accompany the chord charts. Musicians (including beginners) can use this section to learn the chanting tunes that will enhance their spiritual practices.

Brighter Than the Sun
issued in 2003 and remastered and reissued in 2007

1. Brighter Than the Sun
A song inspired by meditation and which will hopefully encourage others to practice it.

```
C
I sit in silence and hear an inner sound.
F              C  GC
I feel God's presence, all around.
C
My heart and His become as one,
F             C     G     C
Merging together we are brighter than the sun.
```

I open my eyes and feel a gentle breeze,
Rustling the bushes it's the wind in the trees.
Watching the people walk and run,
I see Him again, He's brighter than the sun.

Walking to work, I smell some baking bread,
Rising in an oven in a nearby shed.
Imagining the taste of a freshly baked bun,
I feel Him again, He's brighter than the sun.

Sunset has come and I close my eyes.
I go deep inside to find that inner light.
Deeper and deeper, I am nearly done,
I find Him again, He's brighter than the sun.

Come with me and close your eyes,
Go deep inside and find that inner light.
Deeper and deeper, and one by one,
He's right there inside of you, He's brighter than the sun.
Deeper and deeper, and one by one,
He's right there inside of us, He's brighter than the sun

Song link: https://youtu.be/SqDsh1hjWRk

2. Common Home
An ecological song to be sung on Earth Day, or any other day for that matter.

G
We're tearing apart our mother Earth,
C   G
Like some dogs a'fighting for a dry old bone.
G
When will we learn to do it right,
D   C D G
And have some respect for our common home.

Rivers and valleys, mountains and streams,
These are some of our most precious dreams.
We've got to treat them as our very own,
And have some respect for our common home.

Birds and trees and insects, you and me,
Each of us has a right to be.
I think that it's time to make this known,
And have some respect for our common home.

There's enough in this world for each one's need,
But not enough for each one's greed.
I think that it's time to make this known,
And have some respect for our common home.

It's not enough to sit here and sing this song.
Let's wake the world, taking everyone along.
I think that it's time to make this known
And have some respect for our common home.

Song link: https://youtu.be/Cb0ZddlNOXk

3. For Everyone
The whole universe is the common property of humanity, a big concept in a simple song.

```
D
Does Anyone own the sun,
C       G       D
Can anyone claim the moon?
D
I think it's plain to see
C         G       D
That they shine for you and me,
C  G  D        C  G D
And Everyone, For Everyone
C  G  D        C  G D
For you and me, For Everyone
```

The early bird's morning call
The Summer's gentle rain
Fall on one and all
Treating everyone the same.
They're for you and me, and Everyone
For you and me, For everyone

This great big universe
Belongs to every one of us.
From a tiny speck of sand
To a giant galaxy
It's for you and me, and Everyone.
For you and me, For Everyone.

Does Anyone own the sun,
Can anyone claim the moon?
I think it's plain to see
That they shine for you and me,
And Everyone, For Everyone
For you and me, For Everyone

Song link: https://youtu.be/RSdMJenZF64

4. Till I Found You
This is an autobiographical song. The second verse is literally true.

```
E                     A                 E
I Woke up one morning, I knew it was time to leave.
E              A    B7    E
I packed up my bag, and hit that open road.
E                       A                  E
I didn't know what I wanted, but was looking for something new.
E              A   B7     E
Never thought I'd get it, till I found You.
```

I went to the west, and I went to the east.
Someone pointed me north, and after that I headed south.
I Stopped in the middle, I didn't know what to do.
Couldn't get salvation, till I found You.

```
E              A           E
Everlasting love, everlasting bliss
E            A      B7                        E
Everlasting You, making my dreams come true.
E         E          A     B7      E
I'm walking on the path of bliss, now that I've found You.
E                 A   B7   E
Couldn't get salvation till I found You.
E                          A    B7    E
I'm walking on the path of bliss, since I found You.
```

Song link: https://youtu.be/YOJrS5pDZ4g

Note for beginning guitarists: If you are having trouble making or changing to the B7 chord. Put a capo on fret two and then play a D instead of E, a G instead of A and an A or A7 instead of B7.

5. In the Stillness of the Morning

Another song about meditation. It ends with the mantra "Baba Nam Kevalam" which means "love is all there is."

```
D                         G    D
In the stillness of the morning I long for You,
D           A   D
I call Your name over again.
G    A D G A D
Come to me set me free.
```

I go inside to that inner place,
I long to gaze at your smiling face.
Now I see, You're here with me.

I offer my all at Your lotus feet.
My love is true, as I merge with You.
My love is true, as I merge with You.

In the stillness of the morning I long for You,
Come to me set me free.

Song link: https://youtu.be/MI-no3NuabA

6. I Can Never Be Apart From You

About the omnipresence of the Supreme One (or your loved one)

```
D             G    A   D
You're the silence in the center of a storm,
D             G    A    D
You're the fire that keeps my heart warm
        G      A       D
You're watching everything that I do
        G    A      D
I can never be apart from You.
```

You're the love in the air that I breathe.
You're the fragrance that floats in the breeze.
I see you in the many and the few,
I can never be apart from You.

You're the sound of the mighty ocean's roar.
You're the calm in the midst of a war.
I feel your presence through and through,
I can never be apart from You.

Song link: https://youtu.be/D4UQ7xY_-7U

7. Crimson Dawn

A song about the coming of humanity's bright future

```
   E                    A
I'm waiting for a new day's light,
             B7        E
I 'm hoping for a future that's bright.
   E                    A
I'm watching a new world being born,
             B7        E
Soon I'm gonna see a crimson dawn.
```

This world is big enough for all,
It's just that our minds are too small,
To see the beauty of all things,
And the happiness that harmony brings.

I'm waiting for a new day's light,
I 'm hoping for a future that's bright.
I'm watching a new world being born,
Soon I'm gonna see a crimson dawn.

I think it's time to live and let live,
Stop grabbing, start learning how to give.
How long will it take for us to know,
That the secret of life is letting go?

I'm waiting for a new day's light,
I 'm hoping for a future that's bright.
Soon I'm gonna see a crimson dawn.

Song link: https://youtu.be/HhnNrUCV6RU

8. As the Word Spins Around

A song of social justice, dedicated to the less vocal people of the world, those who are struggling to survive.

```
D            C  D              C  D
There're some people in this world without any voice.
D            C  D              C  D
There's some people in this world without any choice.
        C  G     D    C  G  D
And they toil day and night, stuck in their plight,
        C  G  D              C    G  D
As the world spins around, as the world spins around.
D  C  D  C  D  C  D
La la la la la la la la la la la la la la
```

There're some people in this world, taking everything.
And they never stop to think, what their actions will bring,
As the world spins around, as the world spins around.

There're some people in this world,
With a spark in their soul,
And they hear the other's cries,
And they're ready to arise,
As the world spins around, as the world spins around

Come on people of this world.
We've got to change this place,
Bringing happiness and joy,
To all the human race, to all the human race,
As the world spins around, as the world spins around.

Song link:

https://www.youtube.com/watch?v=F0ePT1LDlKY

9. I Don't Eat Meat
Gives the reasons why it is good to be a vegetarian.

```
G                    C    D  G
Animals are my friends and I treat them right.
G                    C       D G
I spare their lives, eating veggies and rice.
C   D  G     C   D  G
I don't eat meat, I don't eat flesh,
    C   D G    C D G
I'm trying to do my very best.
```

My body is strong and my mind is clear.
So tell everybody far and near, that
I don't eat meat, I don't eat flesh
I'm trying to do my very best.

I'm not too thin, and I'm not to fat.
My veggie diet is where its at.
So tell every body in the east and the West,
That I don't eat meat, I don't eat flesh.

Our mother planet is very small.
Let's use everything for the good of all
that's why I don't eat meat, I don't eat flesh
I'm trying to do my very best.

Song link: https://youtu.be/sjQLIoIF9rw

10. Rainbow of Humanity
There is only one race, the human race. This idea is set to music.

```
E              A    E
Everybody laughs when they're glad,
A    E    B7         E
Everybody cries when they're sad.
E              A    E
I don't care what the people may say,
A    E    B7         E
I know there's only one human race.
A    E    B7   E
Brother sister can't you see
A    E    B7 E
We're all one big family,
             A    E  B7 E
We're the rainbow of humanity.
```

We're all breathing the same planet's air,
And everyone one has a right to their share.
Red or yellow, black or white,
It's time to put an end to this useless fight.
Brother sister can't you see
We're all one big family,
We're the rainbow of humanity.

I'm waiting for a better day,
When everyone will see it this way.
I don't know how long it will be,
Till we all live in harmony,
As the Rainbow of Humanity,
We'll live like one big family, 'cause
We're the Rainbow of Humanity.

Song link: https://youtu.be/39IQuE7Zmw4

11. One Fine Day I'm gonna go with a smile

Based on a poem by the Indian poet Tulsi Das who said that people come into the world crying, as the onlookers smile. He said that we should leave the world with a smile, after having done a lot of good work, and that we should let the others cry.

```
D              G     D G    D  A     D
I came to this world, one fine day, one fine day, one fine day.
D              G     D G    D  A     D
I came with a cry as the others smiled one fine day, one fine day.
G     D     A     D G    D  A     D
One fine day, One fine day, One fine day, I came with a cry.
```

I started to learn the lessons of life, one fine day, one fine day.
I learned how to give with all of might, one fine day, one fine day.
One fine day, One fine day, One fine day, I learned how to give.

I gave what I could to all that I could, One fine day, One fine day.
I tried to do go for as long as I could, One fine day, One fine day.
One fine day, One fine day, One fine day, I did what I could.

I'm gonna leave this world, one fine day, one fine day, one fine day.
I'm gonna go with a smile and let the others cry, one fine day, one fine day.
One fine day, One fine day, One fine day, I gonna leave with a smile
One fine day, One fine day, One fine day, I gonna go with a smile.

Song link: https://youtu.be/2Ts37ZllRmE

12. The Wise Ones Say

An Indian proverb says that we should do good things immediately, but we should delay doing anything that is bad. Good advice.

```
E               A       E
I went through life losing my way,
               B7              E
making mistakes with each passing day.
         A       B7    E
Then I stopped and looked around,
A         B7   E
and this is what I found:
E                       A   E
If you've got something good, do it today.
E                  B7    E
Gonna do something bad, make a delay.
A          B7      E
This is what the wise one's say.
```

I forgot the good advice and got stuck again.
I found myself in a terrible jam.
Then I listened to a little bird,
And this is what I heard:

If you've got something good, do it today.
Gonna do something bad, make a delay.
This is what the wise one's say.

Another day came and another day went,
I finally learned what the good message meant.
Then I made a fateful choice,
To listen to my inner voice, saying:

If you've got something good, do it today.
Gonna do something bad, make a delay.
This is what the wise one's say..

Song link: https://youtu.be/e3uros7U5ps

13. Forever and Ever

A spiritual love song. Sing it to God, or to your nearest and dearest.

```
D
Drench me with the tears of love,
C                        D
Hold me close and never, never leave me.
D                   C
Shower me with your perfect peace,
G        A
Forever and ever.
```

I'm adrift on the sea of life,
Floating further, further from the shoreline.
Pick me up and give me shelter in Your smile.
Hold me close and keep me here all the while,
Forever and ever.

To be with You is my last desire.
Take me closer, closer to that moment.
Charm me with the sweetness of Your gentle song.
Let me know I'm in the place where I belong,
Forever and ever.
```
D                 C
Baba Nam Kevalam, Baba Nam Kevalam
D                 C
Baba Nam Kevalam, Baba Nam Kevalam
G        A
Baba Nam Kevalam
```

Song link: https://youtu.be/b5IqFQoT4WA

Love is the Best
Album issued in 2009

1. We are Never Alone or Helpless

The main teaching of yoga is encapsulated in this song, so in a way it is my signature song.

```
G
When the problems of the world lay heavy in your head,
C            G
And you don't know where to turn.
Why don't you go inside and find your inner strength
D         C          G
And remember a lesson we must learn.
G
We are never alone or helpless.
C                               G
The force that guides the stars guides us too.
We are never alone or helpless
D             C            G
The force that guides the stars guides us too.
```

When you're down and out and feeling kind of low,
Don't give up the fight.
Because there's one more thing
I think that you should know.
You're guided by an inner light.

We are never alone or helpless.
The force that guides the stars guides us too.
We are never alone or helpless
The force that guides the stars guides us too.

So start each day with a bouncing stride,
And finish it with a smile.
And if you should ever lose your way,
Remember He's with us all the while

Song links: 1. https://youtu.be/g4xquOgZAXA

2. https://www.youtube.com/watch?v=Yo-ow69S0TM

2. **From Zero to Hero**

This is a song to sing when you're down in spirits, because it will remind you that you have what it takes to pick yourself up.

```
D              G
Don't stay down, erase that frown
D                    A
Your present state is not your fate.
D                      G
There's more to you then you'll ever know.
D        A     D
Reach inside and let it show.
D        A   G           D
From zero to hero, you can make it if you try
D        A   G           D
From zero to hero, grab some wings, we're gonna fly.
```

If you're out today, you'll be in tomorrow,
Kick the blues, say goodbye to sorrow.
Step right up and take your place,
Wow them all with your shining face.

From zero to hero, you can make it if you try.
From zero to hero, keep on singing till you die.

Dry your eyes, forget the bad times.
Lift your chin and learn some new lines.
Start today and make your stand.
It's time to play your winning hand.

From zero to hero, you can make it if you try.
From zero to hero, keep on singing till you die

Song link: https://youtu.be/ti6G4TPMhZA

3. Liberate Your Mind
There are different kinds of dogmas or belief systems that don't allow our minds to expand. We should strive to overcome these boundaries. That is what this song is all about.

```
E
The preacher man says you're living in sin
A
A politician will do you in.
E     B7            E
How's a common man to win?
E
You've got to liberate your mind from fear
      A
The day of freedom is coming near
E     B7     E
Human life is very dear.
```

Someone says God's in the east,
Another one says He's in the west.
How to choose the very best?

You've got to liberate your mind from fear
The day of freedom is coming near
Human life is very dear.

Someone says, "I hate the others,
Dark skin men can't be our brothers."
When will we love one another?

You've got to liberate your mind from fear
The day of freedom is coming near
Human life is very dear.

The preacher man says you're born in sin
A politician will do you in.
How's a common man to win?

You've got to liberate your mind from fear

The day of freedom is coming near
Human life is very dear.

Song link: https://youtu.be/AfpM1QyuOFo

4. I Know You Can't Be Far

The Supreme Being, the "You" in this song, is not far away from you or me.

```
G               C           G              D
```
You came upon a long dark night. You came to ease my mind.
```
G                            C
```
Now the clouds are gone and my soul's at peace
```
G         D      G
```
I'm waiting for another time.
```
C             G        D           G
```
Are you hiding in the moonlight, dancing on a distant star?
```
C          G       Am          D
```
Are you right inside my heart? I know you can't be far.

You lit my world with a flood of light, lifted me from my gloom,
I don't know when I will see you again,
But I am hoping that you come back soon.

Are you hiding in the moonlight, dancing on a distant star?
Are you right inside my heart? I know you can't be far.

You took my hand and led me along, a path so straight and true,
I can't forget what you did for me, my thoughts race back to you.

Are you hiding in the moonlight, dancing on a distant star?
Are you right inside my heart? I know you can't be far.

Song link: https://youtu.be/gUcPXTUYCA4

5. I'm Waiting for that Time

This song expresses my dream for what the world could one day be.

```
Am                        G          Am
```
I'm waitin' for that time, yes I'm waiting for that time,
```
Am                        G          Am
```
I'm waitin' for that time, yes I'm waiting for that time,
```
G                         F     C
```
When good folks will hold their heads up high
```
G                                F      C
```
And hungry kids will never pierce the night with their cry,

I'm waitin' for that time, yes I'm waiting for that time,
I'm waitin' for that time, yes I'm waiting for that time,
When we'll judge a man by what he does,
And not for who his father was.

I'm waitin' for that time, yes I'm waiting for that time,
I'm waitin' for that time, yes I'm waiting for that time,
When we'll love one another regardless of race,
And go pitch our tents in any old place.

I'm waitin' for that time, yes I'm waiting for that time,
I'm waitin' for that time, yes I'm waiting for that time,

When we'll share the earth's bounty fair and square
And watch the world blooming everywhere

I'm waitin' for that time, yes I'm waiting for that time,
I'm waitin' for that time, yes I'm waiting for that time.

Song link: https://youtu.be/ydfpwuYoRn8

6. A Better Deal

Here is a song explaining why I am a vegetarian.

```
G                                C            G
I've got some bread on my table, salad on my plate.
G                                Am           D
I just drank some juice and I'm feeling really great.
G                           C            G
I don't know why we have to kill for our meal.
G                           Am D  G
Let's give our furry friends a better deal
```

Watermelon, cantaloupe, cherries or lime,
I'm eating all these things and I'm feeling really fine.
I don't know why we have to kill for our meal.
Let's give our furry friends a better deal.

Carrots, potatoes, tofu and peas,
Cook them all together and you'll get what you need.
I don't know why we have to kill for our meal.
Let's give our furry friends a better deal.

Let's give our feathered friends a better deal.
Let's give our finny friends a better deal.
Let's give all living beings a better deal, a better deal.

Song link: https://youtu.be/tGBotu9zBj4

7. My Heart Will Go on Loving You

Just a love song, or it can be a spiritual love song too.

Capo on 4th fret

```
C            F        C       G
Neither dust nor haze can cover my gaze.
C            F        C       G
Nor can snow or sleet slow my feet.
C            F        C       G
If the wind cries out with a lonely tune,
F.                    G       C
Still my heart will go on loving you,
             F        G       C
Yes my heart will go on loving you.
```

Let the good and bad times come my way.
I'll be all right on any day.
In joyous crowd or in solitude
Still my heart will go on loving you.
Yes my heart will go on loving you.

I'll walk this road with its ups and downs.
I'll wear a smile not a frown.
Whether skies are gray or skies are blue
Still my heart will go on loving you
Yes my heart will go on loving you.

Song link: https://youtu.be/BBDkDrhb9ws

8. Open My Heart

This is a spiritual doo-wop song. The love interest for me at least is the Supreme Being.

Capo 2nd Fret

```
G
You're the fountain of my life,
C        D
The source of my might.
 G
You sweep away the darkness
C        D
With a burst of light.
G C    G    D
Open my heart wide,
G C    G    D
Take me by your side.
```

You're the pillar of mind,
The hope of my heart.
You wake me from my slumber,
Help me make a new start

Open my heart wide
Take me by your side.

You're a tower of love,
A fortress of peace.
You wash away my worries,
Set my soul free.
Open my heart wide
Take me by your side.

Song link: https://youtu.be/CiYAocOa2w4

9. Love is the Best
lyrics by Gustavo Monje and Dada Veda
This started out as a children's songs, for kids in our kindergarten in Albania, and expanded to be a song for kids of all ages.
Capo 4th fret

```
D                    G
I was walking down my street
D                    G
Looking for folks to greet.
D                    G
Skipping through the park,
D           G
Happy as a lark

C         G     D
Then I looked up to the sky
C         G       D
Watching the birds on high
C              G      D
And I knew it was time to fly
              G
That's why, I love you,
D   G   D   G
I love me, I love you
D   G
I love me
C  G  D    C  G  D
Love is the Best, Love is the Best
```

I was sailing through the seas
Catching the ocean's breeze
Twisting with the wind,
Watching he clouds roll in.
Then I saw your shining face,
Breaking through the haze,
Brightening up my days

That's why, I love you,

I love me, I love you
I love me
Love is the Best, Love is the Best

I was strumming on my guitar
Gazing at a distant star
Humming a simple tune
and hoping to see you soon.
Then I heard your calling song,
Carrying me along with your love so strong.
That's why, I love you, I love me, I love you, I love me
Love is the best, Love is the Best

Song link: https://youtu.be/n1UpV40PtFU

10. Good Old Kiirtan Baba Nam Kevalam

"Baba Nam Kevalam" is a meditation mantra and it means "Love is all there is." Sing along with the CD and then sit silently with your eyes closed and back straight. As you sit in silence keep thinking "Baba Nam Kevalam" and feel love within you and all around you. This recording is in the key of D.

D   A   D
Baba Nam Kevalam
A   G   D
Baba Nam Kevalam

Song link: https://youtu.be/ybfUqXrAHyo

As the World Spins Around
released May 2011

1. As the World Spins Around

Billions of people on this planet live on two dollars a day or less. This song is about their plight as well as the responsibility of the rest of us to do something about it.

Capo on 4th Fret to match the key in this recording

```
D              C   D        C   D
There're some people in this world without any voice.
D              C   D        C   D
There's some people in this world without any choice.
C   G      D   C   G   D
And they toil day and night, stuck in their plight
C   G   D          C   G   D
As the world spins around, as the world spins around.
D   C   D   C   D   C D C
La la la la la la la la la la la la la la
```

There're some people in this world, taking everything.
And they never stop to think, what their actions will bring
As the world spins around, as the world spins around.

There're some people in this world
With a spark in their soul,
And they hear the other's cries,
And they're ready to arise,
As the world spins around, as the world spins around

Come on people of this world.
We've got to heal this place,
Bringing happiness and joy,
To all the human race, to all the human race,
As the world spins around, as the world spins around.

Song link: https://youtu.be/2iQm8IZneu0

2. Precious Kind of Love

Love makes the whole world go around, no doubt about it. A person's love for the Supreme One is indeed a very precious kind of love.

```
E                        A
```
I'm feeling a special kind of feeling.
```
E                        B7
```
There's a glow of peace in my soul
```
E                  A
```
My heart wants to sing a song of love
```
E       B7      E
```
Now I'm finally whole

```
E                        A
```
It's a precious kind of love,
```
E                 B7
```
Love of the most Beloved.
```
E                        A
```
It's a precious kind of love,
```
E            B7   E
```
Love of the most Beloved.

My thoughts take me higher and higher,
To a place beyond the sky.
I'm bathing in a sea of bliss,
It's a love no one can deny.

It's a precious kind of love,
Love of the most Beloved.
It's a precious kind of love,
Love of the most Beloved.

There's nothing much more to ask for.
Nothing much more to crave.
I'm riding a surge of devotion,
Surfing on a Cosmic Wave.

It's a precious kind of love,
Love of the most Beloved.

It's a precious kind of love,
Love of the most Beloved.

Song link: https://youtu.be/0A4W0XNFXJ0?si=_Ckh_K_C6X86cv2V

3. Now I See You
A mystical song about chasing after the elusive One who is playing hide and seek with the universe.

```
D                    G      D
I woke up this morning looking for you.
D                    A      D
Could find no trace I was feeling so blue.
D                    G      D
Searched the forest, searched the glen,
D                    A      D
Wondering when I would see you again.
G      D       A      D
But then I saw you in my mind
G         D    A   D
With a loving gaze oh so kind.

D              G    D
Now I see you, now I don't
D              A    D
Now I see you, now I don't.
D
I know you'll love me
G          D
Don't say you won't.
D              A    D
Now I see you, now I don't
```

You're hiding in the sky so wide,
I'm chasing after, don't care for my pride.
I thought I saw you on the ocean floor,
I plunged within looking for more
I'm gonna catch you, just wait and see
I'll stick around to eternity.

Now I see you, now I don't
Now I see you, now I don't.
I know you'll love me
Don't say you won't.
Now I see you, now I don't

Why are you playing hide and seek
When all I want is just one peek?
I'm trying to follow your every move,
But you slip away, I can't find the groove.
I'm not going to give up, I'm not going to quit.
Gonna plant my heart in the place where you sit.

Now I see you, now I don't
Now I see you, now I don't.
I know you'll love me
Don't say you won't.
Now I see you, now I don't
Now I see you, now I don't.
Now I see you….

Song link: https://youtu.be/xTcBIMZ_7e0?si=2iQpUiQ8E6dMNoBi

4. Make Me Humble

500 years ago a yogi in Bengal India Chaitanya Mahaprabhu gave a few words of advice on how to live an ideal life. Those words of advice form the lyrics of this song.

Capo on the third fret

```
G                         C              D        G
Look at everybody walking on the grass yet it pops up once again.
G                         C              D G
It bears the steps and crushing weight without any end.
C         D           G                Em
I've got to be just as strong, you know I'm going to carry on.
```

So,
```
C            D
Make me humble like the grass
G          Em
I'll be as tolerant as a tree
C            D
I'll give respect to all I see
G          Em
I'll sing your name endlessly
```
Look at the trees giving everything, asking nothing in return.
Fruit and flowers for everyone, it's a lesson I'm gonna learn.
So,

Make me humble like the grass
I'll be as tolerant as a tree
I'll give respect to all I see
I'll sing your name endlessly

Look at everybody saluting the rich, and the pretty ones too.
But take a look around you for that poor boy next to you.
Give him respect and dignity, it's the only thing we gotta do.
So,

Make me humble like the grass
I'll be as tolerant as a tree
I'll give respect to all I see
I'll sing your name endlessly

Oh Lord, you gave me a voice and I'm singing just for you.
I'm gonna sing every day and night, my whole life through.
So,

Make me humble like the grass
I'll be as tolerant as a tree
I'll give respect to all I see
I'll sing your name endlessly

Song link: https://youtu.be/j9GU4yuYqAw?si=Ij_2OvKgVviddAcJ

5. No More Blood, No More Tears
A plea for world peace based on the words of the late Yitzhak Rabin who said, on the White House lawn in 1993, "Enough of blood, enough of tears."

```
C                       F
I'd like to make the bitter sweet,
C                       G
Trying to see the world complete.
C                           F
Sometimes I wonder when the job will be done
C         G         C
we'll fix this globe for everyone.
F                   C
```

There'll be no more blood, no more tears
```
G            C
```
An end to strife an end to fear.
```
F                   C
```
There'll be no more blood, no more tears
```
G            C
```
An end to strife an end to fear.

Can't you see we missed the boat
We're in the deep and must sink or float.
Some say it will always be like this
But I don't buy it and continue to wish

For no more blood, no more tears
An end to strife an end to fear.

The raging storm will one day end,
The long time foe will be our friend.
In a bit of time we'll se the light
Sort the mess and set everything right.

There'll be no more blood, no more tears
An end to strife and end to fear.

Song link: https://youtu.be/3ICk-7XXNpY?si=Xn4xSrK7V07oOzfd

6. It's the System

It's not the economy that is troubling people everywhere; it is the economic system itself that is the problem. This song was written during the U.S. presidential elections of 2008.

```
Am                        G            Em
Everybody's wondering why the poor are growing poorer.
Am                   G        Em
Politicians say they're giving more and morer.
Am                        G          Em
People scratch their heads while looking for a reason.
Am                           G      Em
If I tell you the answer, they may try me for treason.
```

```
Am
It's the system people.
        G
It's the system people.
Am
It's the system people.
G
It's the system people
```

Tweedle Dee is running for election
Tweedle Dum says he'll give us some protection.
Nobody is getting to the root of the problems
They're going round in circles, without a solution.

It's the system people.
It's the system people.
It's the system people.
It's the system people

We're traveling together on a tiny green planet.
Continue like this there'll be nothing left on it.
It's time to stop the plunder, the greed and the looting.
It's time for some healing, some caring and some sharing.

It's the system people.
It's the system people.

It's the system people.
It's the system people

You talk about raising the poor from the gutter
but take a look around you at the fat cat's clutter.
He can live without his Rolls Royce and luxury toys
there will be enough for all, for all our girls and boys.

It's the system people.
It's the system people.
It's the system people.
It's the system people

Song link: https://youtu.be/obTVYJxFNbE?si=L6Kh9JV4prfRMyZX

7. Thank You

Did you ever want to thank someone who helped you turn your life around completely? That's what this song is about.

```
D
I've been roaming and I've been rambling,
G              D
I've been scrambling down that road.
D
I've been hoping, I've been moping,
G           D
I've been carrying a heavy load.
G                    A
But I'm not gonna cry out anymore,
G                    A
You gave me what I was looking for
D       G    D
Thank you, thank you
```

I've been thinking and I've been sinking,
I've been struggling to find my way.
I've been searching, I've been yearning,
Waiting for a better day

But I'm not gonna cry out anymore,
You gave me what I was looking for
Thank you, thank you

I've been moaning, I've been groaning
I've been grumbling for oh so long.
I've been falling, I've been stalling.
Wondering what was wrong.

But I'm not gonna cry out anymore,
You gave me what I was looking for
Thank you, thank you

Song link: https://youtu.be/fB8Qv3AYf4Q?si=Heht91TSVLZ70nSy

8. Just Being Good, Is Not Good Enough
We should be good, but not good for nothing. That is what the song is about
Capo on the third fret

```
G                          D
```
I know you follow the rules and are kind to one and all
```
G                          D
```
You're a model sort of guy and you're standing straight and tall.
```
C                     G
```
You're so good to your kids and your puppy dog too.
```
      C            D
```
I've got nothing bad to say about all the things you do.
```
G                          D
```
But who's gonna tame the beasts and speak out for the meek?
```
G                          D
```
And who's gonna tell the brutes their lying days are through?
```
C                     G
```
That's why we're all crying now and times are getting rough
```
C            D
```
and just being good is not good enough.

You say it's not your battle that it's none of your affairs.
You've got better things to do as you hurry down the stairs.
But wait a minute mister you've really got it to see.
This is not the work for others, it's a job for you and me

And who's gonna tame the beasts and speak out for the meek?
And who's gonna tell the brutes their lying days are through?
That's why we're all crying now and times are getting rough
and just being good is not good enough.

What can I say to move you, and wake you from your sleep?
Our ship lies in tatters as we plunge into the deep
Don't look to any other to save us from our plight.
There's no one but you and me on this dark and cloudy night.

And who's gonna tame the beasts and speak out for the meek?
And who's gonna tell the brutes their lying days are through?
That's why we're all crying now and times are getting rough

and just being good is not good enough.

Song link: https://youtu.be/ZLUUmkkG0jk?si=6SvE02Ao1dQRwE3N

9. I'd Really Like to Know

What does it really mean to be "pro-life?" This song, also inspired by the U.S. elections of 2008, looks at the inconsistencies of some politicians.
Capo on sixth fret

```
Am                            G
She don't kill unborn babies, she's above blame
Am                            G
But moose, deer and caribou are her fair game.
F                   E7
Now I just don't get it. I'd really like to know
F                        E7              Am
Why some lives are sacred and others have to go.
```

In 10,000 BC it was cool to kill a beast
Human life depended on some scraps of meat.
But time has moved on and we really need to see
What can we do to stop this killing spree.

And I just don't get it I'd really like to know
Why some lives are sacred and others have to go.

They say that carrying guns is everybody's right
The Founding Fathers said "fight the good fight."
But in our schools kids are dying caught in a blight
Of aimless bullets fired in broad day light.

And I just don't get I'd really like to know
Why some lives are sacred, and others have to go.

They say that carrying guns is everybody's right
The Founding Fathers said "fight the good fight."
But in our streets kids are dying caught in a blight
Of aimless bullets fired in broad day light

And I just don't get I'd really like to know
Why some lives are sacred, and others have to go.

Song link: https://youtu.be/5y9FdTyH-94?si=3fuzp7QsUOPt1-pG

10. Why Should I Worry

I started meditation one day with a whole lot of worries; when I finished they had all vanished and I wrote this song so I could explain it to you.
Capo on fourth fret

```
D                            Bm
Why should I worry when You're here by me?
E                      G
Why should I worry when it's plain to see,
D            Bm             E         G
I've got You and You've got me and we'll be together till eternity.
G    D G    Em   A    D   G    Em    A
Now I'll lay down my heavy load, as I walk on life's winding road
```

I tried so hard, I tried so long, to be a man, oh so strong
Never knew that I had it wrong, for You were with me all along
Now I'll lay down my heavy load, as I walk on life's winding road.

I'm fixing my life gonna do it right. Never going to let You out of my sight.
I'll feel Your love every day and night
My cares dissolve in Your endless light
Now I'll lay down my heavy load, as I walk on life's winding road

Song link: https://youtu.be/YwWIKuwMLXs?si=uR7n5GQtRhSwsoBr

11. Live Kiirtan

Chanting the mantra Baba Nam Kevalam, recorded live in April 2011. Sing along with us. Capo on third fret. There are two tunes.

Tune 1

```
G         C         G            D
Baba Nam Kevalam Baba Nam Kevalam
G         C         G            D
Baba Nam Kevalam Baba Nam Kevalam
     Em        C         G            D
Baba Nam Kevalam Baba Nam Kevalam
     Em        C         G            D
Baba Nam Kevalam Baba Nam Kevalam
```

Tune 2

```
Am        G         F         G    Am
Baba Nam Kevalam Baba Nam Kevalam
Am        G         F         G    Am
Baba Nam Kevalam Baba Nam Kevalam
Am                  G              Am
Baba Nam Kevalam Baba Nam Kevalam
Am                  G              Am
Baba Nam Kevalam Baba Nam Kevalam
Am        G         F         G    Am
Baba Nam Kevalam Baba Nam Kevalam
```

Song Link: https://youtu.be/n3vNowTdE4I?si=yDBhAAKExVJwx1e8

Do What You Can
Released September 1, 2013

Do What You Can Is a collection of songs for children done in a simple folk style by Dada Veda and friends. The title track, Do What You Can, is based on an incident in India's epic poem, The Ramayana, in which a small squirrel shows that it is your heartfelt effort that counts and not your absolute strength.

1. Do What You Can (written by Dada Veda)

```
D                  G     D           A      G      D
Good king Rama was building a bridge, building a bridge, building a bridge
D                  G     D       G       A    D
Good king Rama was building a bridge one bright and sunny day.
D                         G    D    G    A    G     D
Some monkeys brought big boulders for that bridge, for that bridge, for that bridge
D                         G    D    G     A     D
Some monkeys brought big boulders for that bridge one bright and sunny day.
D                G     D   G    A    G    D
A squirrel brought a pebble for that bridge, for that bridge, for that bridge
D                G     D    G     A    D
A squirrel brought a pebble for that bridge one bright and sunny day.

Bm            G         D
So do what you can, whenever you can
G       A       D
No matter what people may say
Bm         G         D
Do what you can whenever you can
G     A   D
Starting from today.
D                    G     D
The monkeys started laughing, ha, ha, ha,
G   A  G   D
ha, ha, ha, ha, ha, ha,
D                    G    D
The monkeys started laughing ha, ha, ha
G       A    D
One bright and sunny day.
The squirrel started crying, boo, hoo, hoo
boo, hoo, hoo, boo hoo hoo
The squirrel started crying, boo, hoo, hoo
One bright and sunny day.
```

But do what you can, whenever you can
No matter what people may say
Do what you can whenever you can

Starting from today.

Good king Rama heard that cry
Heard that cry, heard that cry
Good king Rama heard that cry

He took the little squirrel in his palm
In his palm, in his palm
He took the little squirrel in his palm
One bright and sunny day.

He said do what you can, whenever you can
No matter what people may say
Do what you can whenever you can
Starting from today.

Rama stroked the squirrel on its back
On its back, on its back
Rama stroked the squirrel on its back
One bright and sunny day.

And that's why Indian squirrels have three stripes
Have three stripes, have three stripes
And that's why Indian squirrels have three stripes
Ever Since that day.

So do what you can, whenever you can
No matter what people may say
Do what you can whenever you can
Starting from today.

Song link: https://www.youtube.com/watch?v=U6hGKVF3Sng

2. The Wise Ones Say (written by Dada Veda)

The Wise Ones Say
An Indian proverb says that we should do good things immediately, but we should delay doing anything that is bad. Good advice.

```
E         A        E
I went through life losing my way,
                         B7           E
making mistakes with each passing day.
            A         B7      E
Then I stopped and looked around,
A     B7    E
and this is what I found:
E                         A    E
If you've got something good, do it today.
E                B7      E
Gonna do something bad, make a delay.
A          B7         E
This is what the wise one's say.
```

I forgot the good advice and got stuck again.
I found myself in a terrible jam.
Then I listened to a little bird,
And this is what I heard:
If you've got something good, do it today.
Gonna do something bad, make a delay.
This is what the wise one's say.

Another day came and another day went,
I finally learned what the good message meant.
Then I made a fateful choice,
To listen to my inner voice, saying:
If you've got something good, do it today.
Gonna do something bad, make a delay.
This is what the wise one's say.

Song link: https://youtu.be/W8orBso9LFw?si=zWfewdnn88wOMxUD

3. This Little Light of Mine (public domain)
This is an old gospel song. I sing it in kindergartens and in retirement homes.

G
This little light of mine, I'm gonna let it shine.
C
This little light of mine, I'm gonna let it shine
G
This little light of mine, I'm gonna let it shine.
      Em   D   G
Let it shine, let shine, let it shine.

All around the town, I'm gonna let it shine
All around the town, I'm gonna let it shine.
All around the town, I'm gonna let it shine.
Let it shine, let it shine let it shine.

In my daily work, I'm gonna let it shine
In my daily work, I'm gonna let it shine
In my daily work, I'm gonna let it shine
Let it shine, let it shine let it shine.

Hide it under a bushel, No I'm gonna let it shine
Hide it under a bushel No I'm gonna let it shine
Hide it under a bushel No I'm gonna let it shine
Let it shine, let it shine, let it shine.

Spread love around the world, I'm gonna let it shine.
Spread love around the world, I'm gonna let it shine.
Spread love around the world, I'm gonna let it shine.
Let it shine, let it shine, let it shine.

Song link: https://www.youtube.com/watch?v=hlFauYkTQ8U

4. The Eency Weency Spider

This is a popular nursery rhyme usually sung with finger movements matching the adventures of the spider in the song.

```
D                             A        D
The Eency Weensy spider went up the waterspout.
Down came the rain
G              D
And washed the spider out.
Out came the sun
      A        D
And dried up all the rain
                              A        D
And the Eency Weency spider went up the spout again.
```

Capo on the first fret to match the key of the recording

Song link: https://youtu.be/5HbBA-HQrr4?si=_qOocOkHyuYMIfB1

5. Clouds Are Floating

This song comes from the *Circle of Love* songbook and is a song that is sung in Neohumanist Ananda Marga kindergartens around the world. (it uses the same tune as "Frère Jacques" the popular French nursery rhyme)

D
Clouds are floating, clouds are floating
Up so high, up so high
Floating high above us, floating high above us
A   D   A   D
In the sky, in the sky

Song link: https://www.youtube.com/watch?v=lNgMbH1IJY8

6. We Are All Brothers and Sisters Anonymous
This is another song from the Circle of Love songbook.

D
We are all brothers and sisters
G
We are the children of light
D   G
We are the dawn of the future
D   A   D
We are the children of love

Song link: https://www.youtube.com/watch?v=fNFip3ByEUU

7. You Can Make the Sun Shine (written by Singh Kaur)
I first heard this song in 1973 on an album by The Khalsa String Band
Capo on first fret

D
Sing a happy song
C   G   D
Let your love just drift along
D
Shed light on its way
C   G   D
Let it shine from day to day

D   C
You can make the sun shine any old time
G   D
Even when the clouds are there

D   C
You can make the sun shine any old time
G   D
Even when the clouds are there
D   C   G   D
You can make the sun shine
D   C   G   D
You can make the sun shine
D   C
You can make the sun shine any old time
G   D
Even when the clouds are there.
D   C
You can make the sun shine any old time
G   D
Even when the clouds are there.

Song links: https://youtu.be/DjZDacR3TVo?si=_8zah9FCukxw2qFi_

https://youtu.be/l9C_jjC46Kk?si=3Vm94KrCvfGSnomv

Khalsa String Band original version

8. Good Morning Dear Earth, Good Morning Dear Sun (public domain)
This is a circle time favorite in the Waldorf Schools around the world. There are hand and body movements that go along with the song, making it a good exercise.

```
D                         G         D
Good morning dear earth, good morning dear sun
D                         G         A
Good morning dear trees and the flowers everyone.
D                         G         D
Good morning dear bees, and the birds in the trees
     G      D         A       D
Good morning to you and good morning to me.
```

Song link: https://www.youtube.com/watch?v=BkxqIX5hLUA

9. Tiny Green Island P.R. Sarkar

This is song number 68 in the Prabhat Samgiita collection of songs written by P.R. Sarkar from 1982-1990.

Capo on third fret

```
Am          G         F        G       Am
```
I love this tiny green island surrounded by the sea
```
Am          G         F        G       Am
```
I love this tiny green island surrounded by the sea
```
Am                    G
```
Touched by the sea, decorated by sea
```
Am                    G
```
Touched by the sea, decorated by sea
```
Am          G         F        G       Am
```
I love this tiny green island surrounded by the sea.
```
Am
```
Am I a secluded figure?
In the vast, a little, a meager?
Am I a secluded figure?
In the vast, a little, a meager?
```
Am                    G
```
No, no, no, no, I am not alone,
```
Am                    G
```
No, no, no, no, I am not alone,
```
F       G     Am   F     G      Am
```
The Great is with me, the Great is with me.

Song link: https://www.youtube.com/watch?v=fzG6R1e0WH0

10. Love is the Best
(lyrics by Gustavo Monje and Dada Veda)
This song originally appeared as the title song of my second album released in 2009, but an acoustic version appears on this album. It is a song originally written for children, so it is perfect here.
Capo 4th fret

```
D                    G
I was walking down my street
D                    G
Looking for folks to greet.
D                    G
Skipping through the park,
D        G
Happy as a lark

C     G     D
Then I looked up to the sky
C     G        D
Watching the birds on high
C           G    D
And I knew it was time to fly
                G
That's why, I love you,
D   G   D   G
I love me, I love you
D   G
I love me
C   G   D   C   G   D
Love is the Best, Love is the Best
```

I was sailing through the seas
Catching the ocean's breeze
Twisting with the wind,
Watching he clouds roll in.
Then I saw your shining face,
Breaking through the haze,
Brightening up my days
That's why, I love you,

I love me, I love you
I love me
Love is the Best, Love is the Best

I was strumming on my guitar
Gazing at a distant star
Humming a simple tune
and hoping to see you soon.
Then I heard your calling song,
It carry me along with your love so strong.
That's why, I love you, I love me, I love you, I love me
Love is the best, Love is the Best

Song link: https://youtu.be/UMEJJvzQkKk?si=SeanLwddraHAuy2u

11. Love is All There Is/Baba Nam Kevalam

Here is an English and Sanksrit rendition of the Baba Nam Kevalam mantra which I often sang with kids in the kindergarten in Albania.

```
D                C            D
Baba Nam Kevalam Love is all there is.
D                C            D
Baba Nam Kevalam Love is all there is
D                C            D
Baba Nam Kevalam Love is all there is…
D                C            D
Baba Nam Kevalam, Baba Nam Kevalam…
```

Song link: https://www.youtube.com/watch?v=Oa5S1ZZy10g

Trickle On Down
released May 20, 2016

This was my fourth album and as I said in the liner notes, "My main job in life is teaching meditation and yoga, but my musical activities are an important extension of this work…In these short songs I have tried to infuse the eternal truths that are at the core of who we are as individuals and as a society."

1. Trickle on Down

"Trickle on Down," is a lively tune that tells the story of global economic inequality, or as Dada writes, the song is "modern economics explained in 4 ½ minutes."

```
G                             C
Let's fight for the rights of the wealthiest few
G                             D
One day, who knows, we may get there too.
            G                 C
Some say greed is good, and greed is great
     G              D         G
So grab what you can before it's too late.
```

```
G    C    D    G
Trick, trick, trickle on down,
          C       D       G
Trickle on down to you and me
G    C    D    G
Trick, trick, trickle on down,
G         C         D         G
It's a fairy tale you'll never ever see.
```

Don't worry if the loot goes right to the top
It's gonna trickle down to water your crops
Let the poor of the world stand up on their feet
Even though we know they're already beat.

Trick, trick, trickle on down,
Trickle on down to you and me
Trick, trick, trickle on down,
It's a fairy tale you'll never ever see.

I went to school and studied the books
And found our dreams have been stolen by crooks
I traveled the world and met lots of folks
Most of them were already broke.

Trick, trick, trickle on down,

Trick, trick, trickle on down,
It's a fairy tale you'll never ever see.

https://www.youtube.com/watch?v=xsi5_tFeJgk&list=RDxsi5_tFeJgk&start_radio=1

2. The Secret of it All

A song based on the yogic ideal of being striving to be content as much as possible.
Capo on fret 2 (optional)

```
G                    C
I did my work and I'm resting still
D              C       G
No need to chase for one more thrill
G                    C
I am happy as a dog wagging his tail.
D                C   G
With a life like this how can I fail?

G                         Am
'Cause the secret of it all is to know when to stop
     C         G
And be content with what you've got.
```

I'm not gonna run after more and more
I've got some time to rest on the shore.
Some folks rush around like busy bees
They're never happy and never pleased.

'Cause the secret of it all is to know when to stop
and be content with what you've got.

So do your thing but remember to chill
You don't have to keep climbing that hill
No need to scramble near and far
Just take some time and gaze at the stars

'Cause the secret of it all is to know when to stop
and be content with what you've got.

Song link: https://youtu.be/K-Wb6CovDqk?si=K-GE3cRA83dZBKzo

3. Better Than That

Everyone makes mistakes but it's good to reach out and patch things up, before it's too late.

```
E
For many days I thought of me
                    B7      E
I hurt you so but I couldn't see.
E
I've grown a lot since that time
                        B7         E
Working so hard just to change your mind.
     A           E
So dry your tears and start to laugh
A            E
Years ago I was wearing a mask
A            B7         E
But don't you know, I'm better than that.
```

If I could change the bad old days
I'd write the story in another way.
Let's take a chance to start anew
Can't you see there's so much to do.

So dry your tears and start to laugh
Years ago I was wearing a mask
But don't you know, I'm better than that.

We're here today and gone so fast
Can't end it all stuck in the past.
Let's pick up our things and move together
We've got to forget the stormy weather.

So dry your tears and start to laugh
Years ago I was wearing a mask
But don't you know, I'm better than that.

Song link: https://youtu.be/-4CWQlR7EuY?si=CoRZhdJemqYDnsav

4. Spiritual Oasis

"Spiritual Oasis" describes a particular place, a retreat center in Croatia, but it can be any place where good people come together in the spirit of brotherhood and sisterhood.
Capo on fret 2

G
In your rolling green fields and forest trees
That's the place where I want to be.
C
Gazing at all the smiling, friendly faces
G
You are my spiritual oasis.
    D   C   G
Baba Nam Kevalam, Baba Nam Kevalam
G
Let's sing for the future, let's sing for now
Let's dance as the wind flies through the boughs.
C
Though i have been around to many beautiful places
G
You are my spiritual oasis.
    D   C   G
Baba Nam Kevalam, Baba Nam Kevalam

We'll break some bread, we'll share some joy
We'll play like children with a bright new toy
let's gather all around in warm embraces
You are my spiritual oasis.
Baba Nam Kevalam, Baba Nam Kevalam

You're the friend of one you're the friend of all
Let's stand together, so straight and tall
We'll reach for joy and enjoy His graces
You are my spiritual oasis.
Baba Nam Kevalam, Baba Nam Kevalam

Song link: https://youtu.be/lox6iRwQZpk?si=CulQpDIzJvYIHPo0

5. Shower of Grace

Love is pouring down on everyone. Some feel it and some don't. Remove your ego umbrella and you will be drenched in the 'Shower of Grace'.

Em
I was looking for something special
And I searched from place to place
                            C
Life was filled with pain and sorrow
       D   Em
Which I never could erase.
Em   D   Em
Where is the shower of Grace?
Em   D   Em
Where is the shower of Grace?

I traveled around and heard the sound
People talking of time and space
They spoke of God, they spoke of love.
But I couldn't find a trace.

Where is the shower of Grace?
Where is the shower of Grace?
D   Em
People run around, saying that they've got bliss
D   Em
I just know something is amiss
D   Em
Love is there for everyone to see
D   Em
Oh Lord, what about me?

It rang like a bell when somebody said.
"Throw away your ego umbrella
Let your vanity fly into the wind and
You'll see love's real face."
You'll feel the shower of Grace

Song link: https://youtu.be/AT7t-JZRusk?si=lYnOt8IuZbEeSGbd

6. Waiting for That Time

We all have dreams about what we would like to see in the future. "Waiting for that Time" describes my dream of a world where "good folks hold their heads up high and hungry kids never pierce the night with their cry."

```
Am                      G              Am
I'm waitin' for that time, yes I'm waiting for that time,
Am                      G              Am
I'm waitin' for that time, yes I'm waiting for that time,
G                    F        C
When good folks will hold their heads up high
G                              F            C
And hungry kids will never pierce the night with their cry,
```

I'm waitin' for that time, yes I'm waiting for that time,
I'm waitin' for that time, yes I'm waiting for that time

When we'll judge a man by what he does,
And not for who his father was.

I'm waitin' for that time, yes I'm waiting for that time,
I'm waitin' for that time, yes I'm waiting for that time
When we'll love one another regardless of race,
And go pitch our tents in any old place.

I'm waitin' for that time, yes I'm waiting for that time,
I'm waitin' for that time, yes I'm waiting for that time
When we'll share the earth's bounty fair and square
And watch the world blooming everywhere

I'm waitin' for that time, yes I'm waiting for that time,
I'm waitin' for that time, yes I'm waiting for that time

Song link: https://youtu.be/czWbrw7UccE?si=80gvEfLt62T8jz3L

7. Drift in Bliss

This song is based on a poem by the 18th Century Bengali mystic poet Ramprasad Sen.

```
D                   G         D
Whatever you think or do forget Him never.
                            G       D
Keep His name in your heart, now and forever,
      G    A    D        G    A    D
And endlessly active drift in bliss, endlessly active drift in bliss.
```

Put your hands to work but keep your mind on Him.
Tackle all your tasks through thick and thin.
And endlessly active drift in bliss, endlessly active drift in bliss.

Make every minute count, life is so fleeting.
Work for one and all while your heart is beating,
And endlessly active drift in bliss, endlessly active drift in bliss.

Complete all worldly calls, soon as you can.
But don't forget your place in the greater plan,
And endlessly active drift in bliss, endlessly active drift in bliss.

Song link: https://youtu.be/CRlq8reMXRs?si=4J0SAK2SDejT55il

8. Promised Land

This song is a fleeting vision of world where people enjoy a life of bliss. A place that is almost too good to be true.
Capo on fret 4

```
Am                  F      E7           Am
I was wandering in the desert, searching in the sands
F       E7      Am
Trying to find my way.
Am                  F         E7           Am
I was climbing up a mountain, rolling down a hill
F           E7      Am
Trying not to go astray.
F        E7       F           E7
Then I saw You. You took be my hand.
F        E7                Am
Then you led me to the promised land.
```

I was watching everybody, dancing around, enjoying their life of bliss
I thought I was dreaming or maybe in a trance
I felt something was amiss.
Then you held me, and made me understand,
that I was gazing at the promised land.

I didn't want to go back; I didn't want to leave.
I felt my vision slipping away.
I was trying to remember and hold on tight.
I really, really wanted to stay.
Then You told me, grab everybody's hand,
And lead them to the promised land.

Song link: https://youtu.be/bb7GtRCF3ps?si=8nGkVVyR2a1iFS7G

9. I See Your Smile

The Supreme Being can be found permeating every particle of this universe, that's the main idea of this song.
Capo on fret 6

```
G     D         C         G
You lie hidden in the things of the world
              D         C         G
In the suns, the galaxies, the cosmos unfurled
          Em            C    D
In the crying baby and the little child.
Em          D        G
Everywhere I look I see your smile.
```

All that I have and all that I touch
Surely is made of your divine stuff.
The tools of my trade, the blocks of wood
They're simply divine and wonderfully good.

Moving around, from place to place
My hands and feet stay in sacred space
Long may I flow and seek the truth
Let it go on till I merge with You

Song link: https://youtu.be/4oNAWmJejVE?si=VY6imkEindHvuGzf

10. Baba Nam Kevalam

This is a mantra that can be sung before meditation, and even used in silent meditation.
Capo on fret 3

```
Am        G   Am         G   Am
Baba Nam Kevalam, Baba Nam Kevalam
              G          Am
Baba Nam Kevalam, Baba Nam Kevalam
              G          Am
Baba Nam Kevalam Baba Nam Kevalam
                G   F        Am
Baba Nam Kevalam, Baba Nam Kevalam
                G   F        Am
Baba Nam Kevalam, Baba Nam Kevalam
```

Song link: https://youtu.be/ge6O4AI7PXs?si=uAdU8pNVm-m77ibq

Remember the Sun Will Shine
Released January 1, 2018

This was the sixth album, and it featured yoga-infused folk music as well as two songs addressing social concerns.

1. Remember the Sun Will Shine

Even in difficult times we must keep working to build a brighter tomorrow.
Capo on Fret 2

```
G              D         Em      D
There's a battle going on and it's scary no doubt
    G          D          Em     D
And just when you think there's no way out,
C                D
Remember the Sun will shine,
    C            D
For you and me and humankind.
```

Now good beats bad and love trumps hate,
That's why I say it's not too late.
We've got to start working tonight,
We're gonna start working today and tonight.
And

Remember the sun will shine
For you and me and humankind.

One day we'll look back and we will see
That righteous struggle is what we need
To bring out the best in us,
To bring out the best in you and me.
And

Remember the sun will shine
For you and me and humankind.

Song link: https://youtu.be/p6BUDPoqYWk?si=dR0FPx_QfCE_2KWQ

2. It Takes a Caring Heart

Healthcare is a human right, not a privilege of the rich.

```
Am         C        F          E7
A baby is dying, an old man is sighing.
Am         C        F          E7
Here in the U.S. we're not really trying
Am            C        F          E7
To care for the sick and the needy ones too.
F                    E7         Am
We're hoping the market will solve all our blues
             F      E7      F          E7
But, It takes a caring heart and it takes a loving mind
F        E7              F    E7   Am
To hurdle a mountain and heal the wounds of our time.
```

How much does it cost to save all the lives
To fix all the teeth, to check all the eyes?
There's money enough for the bombs and the planes
But when it comes to health it's really a shame.

For, It takes a caring heart and it takes a loving mind
To hurdle a mountain and heal the wounds of our time.

Don't call me a dreamer but life's not for sale
It's not the preserve of the rich and the hale.
we all want to live just as long as we can
but the good old market can't give us a plan

For, it takes a caring heart and it takes a loving mind
To hurdle a mountain and heal the wounds of our time.

Song link: https://youtu.be/xJN8QoV_zcQ?si=IzPgB76UOLr7IeR1

3. Let's Not Wait Till Tomorrow
written by Larry Mitchell
I first heard this from my friend Larry Mitchell in 1973, and I have always loved the spiritual message of this song.

Am7   D   G
There's a little light inside of every one of us.
Am7   D   G
Through the darkness all of us must go.
Am7   D   G   Em
By His grace we'll all get to know Him well.
Am7   D   G
All we got to do is try a little more.

Am7   D   G
So let's not wait till tomorrow.
Am7   D   G
Why not start it today.
Am7   D   G   Em
There's so many little doors to open you know,
Am7   D   G
And He's always there to guide us on our way.

I thought that I had things to do in my life.
Never time to stop and look around.
Sisters and brothers in need of my love,
I guess it's time I gave them what I should.

So, let's not wait till tomorrow.
Why not start it today.
There's so many little doors to open you know,
And He's always there to guide us on our way.

So let's not wait till tomorrow.
Why not start it today.
There's so many little doors to open you know,
And He's always there to guide us on our way.

Song link: https://youtu.be/Y8pr3DE1_rU?si=48IoZRJAJVSJuO92

4. Don't Take It

This is another song in my series of songs about yoga's guide to ethical human conduct. This one is about non-stealing. Another version of this song is included in my album *The Pillars of Yoga*.
Capo on fret 2 (optional)

```
G       C
Don't take it
G          C
You just can't make it
G       C    D       G
You don't need anyone's stuff
G           C
Forget about stealing
G        C
Focus on healing
G     C    D       G
You'll find you've got enough.
```

```
G
What's yours is yours
    Am
And hers is hers
        C           D
No need for anything more
G    C   G    C
Don't take it, you just can't make it
G       C    D       G
You don't need anyone's stuff
```

Come let's enjoy life
Keep away from strife
I know It's gonna work out for sure.
So, sit on the right side
Stay on the bright side
Try and let your spirit soar

What's yours is yours
And hers is hers

No need for anything more
Don't take it, you just can't make it
You don't need anyone's stuff

Don't think about taking it
You can't go on faking it
You'll only tie your mind in a knot
You know I'm not preaching
I'm really just seeking
To find out what's right and what's not.

What's yours is yours
And hers is hers
No need for anything more
Don't take it, you just can't make it
You don't need anyone's stuff

Don't take it, you just can't make it
You don't need anyone's stuff

Song link: https://www.youtube.com/watch?v=BemhudgZwAE

5. Sitting in the Lap of Creation
This song was inspired by my frequent visits to a spiritual center in Poland in the 1990s

```
C                         F     C
From the forest edge I gaze far and wide
                          G      C
Soaking up the peace of the summer sky.
C                    F     C
The buzz of a bee, the rooster's crow.
                              G    C
My heart starts beating because now I know:

              G           F  C
We're in the land of purest emotions
G                    F  C
Filled with those sweet vibrations
              G                       F C
We're heading towards our cosmic destination
G            F    C
We're sitting in the lap of creation.
```

Stately white birch aligned in a row
Tower above the green plains below.
The cows tug the grass
The children run and play
I glance all around and stop when they say:

We're in the land of purest emotions
Filled with those sweet vibrations
We're heading towards our cosmic destination
We're sitting in the lap of creation.

A woodpecker pokes and a bird softly sings.
My heart fills with joy and my soul has wings.
I gaze at the sky and the clouds overhead.
There's beauty all around and that's why it's said:

We're in the land of purest emotions
Filled with those sweet vibrations

We're heading towards our cosmic destination
We're sitting in the lap of creation.

Song link: https://youtu.be/77nT8QAnJbU?si=lX5xJ6FWfeOUnhGn

6. The Lion Sleeps Tonight

This is my version of the pop song that was derived from a song written in South Africa by Soloman Linda. Please look up the lyrics and chords for this song online. The recording on this album was done in the key of D (using chords D, G and A)
Capo on fret 2

Intro chords D, G, D, A

7. Crazy Old Town

This song expresses my amazement at how New York City became a safer place to live, after returning from a 40-year trip around the world.

```
C              F         C       G
Watching the people on the subway oh what a trip

C              F       C        G
Enjoying their lives again without any hitch
F              G
I don't know how it happened
         C     Am
But we can't let it slip
F                     G         C
Because that's the way it's supposed to be
         F              G
And you know it looks so pretty
C                Am
Groovin' on the joyful city
F       G          C
Unfolding our lives in this crazy old town
```

I can go for a ride at a quarter past midnight
I can zip down the street at a quarter to three
I can glide through the park
Even after dark
Because that's the way it's supposed to be

And you know it looks so pretty
Groovin' on the joyful city
Unfolding our lives in this crazy old town

So many different faces from all the world round
Enjoying their lives making one great big sound
With smiles and tears and ups and downs
We're gonna come around
Because that's the way it's supposed to be

And you know it looks so pretty

Groovin' on the joyful city
Unfolding our lives in this crazy old town

And you know it looks so pretty
Groovin' on the joyful city
Unfolding our lives in this crazy old town

Song link: https://youtu.be/80QgQfQzanM?si=Ren5hr65zTbQ7Ucm

8. Do I Need it?

Another ethical precept is the base of this song. Taking more than we need is not good for others and not good for us.

G
I know you've got stuff.
Houses, cars, clothes, gadgets and things
C   G
And you're looking for more, that's for sure.
     D
But do you have need, or is it
C   G
Just your sky-licking greed?

G
If you take too much.
Someone may go homeless, shirtless, toothless, luckless and more.
C   G
That's the way, the way the world works.
D   C   G
I think it's time to cut down on some of those perks.

    D   C
And before you grab anything, ask yourself one time,
G
Do I need it? Do I need it?

So, take what you need.
Get your food, clothes, medicine, shelter and all.
Take what you need, but nothing more.
You'll be happier than you ever were before

And before you grab anything, ask yourself one time,
Do I need it? Do I need it?

Song link: https://youtu.be/PrbPR6dx43c?si=puClh6d1sz9srEWB

9. Be Kind to Everyone

Not-inflicting harm on others is yoga's first ethical principle, and this song expresses this idea in a children's format

```
D            G A D
There goes a little girl in the light
D             G  A D
There runs a little boy, treat him right
G        A     G        A
Don't hurt your brother, don't your sister
G      A     D G D
Be kind to everyone day and night
```

There flies a humming bird oh so nice
I think I see a rabbit in the night
Watch what you say, watch what you do
Be kind to everyone day and night

There jumps a little frog in the creek
Now I see a baby deer oh so sweet.
Spread love to everyone
Go out and have some fun
Be kind to everyone day and night
Day and night

Song link: https://youtu.be/iuV_xIi0YRQ?si=ceMZyZQrVFOQO8JF

10. Crazy Bliss

This is a spiritual love song. We were brainstorming for the theme of a retreat, and I got the idea "crazy bliss." Later on I decided to turn this crazy idea into a song.

Intro chords: G, C, D, C

```
G      C           D   C
What's that feeling coming over me
G      C           D      C
When I gaze into your smiling face?
G              C        D    C
And what's that joy that fills me up
G        C           D        C
When I start to think about your Grace?
G            C   D
Could it be that crazy bliss?
G         C      D    C
It's got to be that crazy bliss.
```

GCDC GCDC (short interlude between verses)
What's that thrill lifts me higher and higher
And opens my heart to a world in woe?
And what's that love that gets me inspired
To share it all with one and all?
Could it be that crazy bliss?
It's got to be that crazy bliss.

Just keep me going until I merge
With You dear one, with You dear one
There's a world out there that I want to serve
And I'll get my strength from a certain place
Could it be that crazy bliss?
It's got to be that crazy bliss.

Song link: https://youtu.be/Dkw8g1w-ULQ?si=o91-kKRmyS0pFCN9

11. Mantra Kiirtan 2011

This is a live recording of mantra chanting kiirtan or kirtan at the Ananda Liina Yoga and Meditation Center in Urbana, IL in 2011. The mantra that is being chanted is Baba Nam Kevalam "only the name of the most Beloved"

The tune is based on my song "In the Stillness of the Morning.

D   G D
Baba Nam Kevalam
D   A   D
Baba Nam Kevalam
G A D   G A D
Baba Nam Kevalam

Song link: https://youtu.be/fv9qUMwNh8Q?si=w2KpXZF77RJV2Uzn

The Pillars of Yoga
released May 15, 2019

This album contains ten songs and each one of them is about one of the ten ethical principles Yama and Niyama that are the base of yoga practice. Some of the songs were recorded on previous albums and some written for this album and all were recorded anew.

1. Be Kind to Everyone

Not-inflicting harm on others is yoga's first ethical principle, and this song expresses this idea in a children's format

```
D            G A D
There goes a little girl in the light
D            G  A D
There runs a little boy, treat him right
G         A    G        A
Don't hurt your brother, don't your sister
G      A     D G D
Be kind to everyone day and night
```

There flies a humming bird oh so nice
I think I see a rabbit in the night
Watch what you say, watch what you do
Be kind to everyone day and night

There jumps a little frog in the creek
Now I see a baby deer oh so sweet.
Spread love to everyone
Go out and have some fun
Be kind to everyone day and night
Day and night

Song link: https://youtu.be/_SabyZUaHLs?si=SSLsyeuNcD_dlk61

2. The Light of Truth

This song expresses the spirit of Satya, using speech, thought and actions in the spirit of welfare. Another way of describing Satya is "benevolent truthfulness"

```
Am                      E7      Am
I want to help everybody under the sun
                             E7     Am
And won't stop working till the job is done
                      Dm
My mind is clear, and my heart is pure
       E7              F       Am
The light of truth shines through my door
```

I'll march along with my head held high
And climb all hills right up to the sky
Gonna stay this course through thick and thin
The light of Truth shines deep within.

```
E7                     F
I speak from heart there's nothing to hide
E7                  F
my outside and inside coincide
Dm              F
I just want to let that inner light
E7        Am
Guide me along
```

Call me a wise one or call me a fool
I won't mind whatever you do
Through good and bad, sun and rain
The light of truth runs in my veins.

Song link: https://youtu.be/YsJhJWMvwQE?si=5gGQhVdbf8NpOkU2

3. Don't Take It
The third element yoga ethics is *Asteya*, not stealing from others. This song expresses the spirit of Asteya.
Capo on fret 2 (optional)

```
G      C
Don't take it
G           C
You just can't make it
G        C    D      G
You don't need anyone's stuff
G           C
Forget about stealing
G        C
Focus on healing
G     C    D      G
You'll find you've got enough.
```

```
G
What's yours is yours
Am
And hers is hers
                    D
No need for anything more
G     C    G     C
Don't take it, you just can't make it
G       C    D      G
You don't need anyone's stuff
```

Come let's enjoy life
Keep away from strife
I know It's gonna work out for sure.
So, sit on the right side
Stay on the bright side
Try and let your spirit soar

What's yours is yours
And hers is hers
No need for anything more

Don't take it, you just can't make it
You don't need anyone's stuff

Don't think about taking it
You can't go on faking it
You'll only tie your mind in a knot
You know I'm not preaching
I'm really just seeking
To find out what's right and what's not.

What's yours is yours
And hers is hers
No need for anything more
Don't take it, you just can't make it
You don't need anyone's stuff

Don't take it, you just can't make it
You don't need anyone's stuff

Song links: https://youtu.be/xJsuhll7T_w?si=UC7L-uGKtzOYn29c

4. I See Your Smile

This song expresses the spirit of *Brahmacarya*, remaining attached to God throughout our worldly activities. According to yogis, every piece of this universe is an expression of God and we should treat people, living beings and even inanimate objects accordingly.

```
D      A         G         D
You lie hidden in the things of the world
                 A        G      D
In the suns, the galaxies, the cosmos unfurled
            Bm          G    A
In the crying baby and the little child.
Bm          A     D
Everywhere I look I see your smile.
```

All that I have and all that I touch
Surely is made of your divine stuff.
The tools of my trade, the blocks of wood
They're simply divine and wonderfully good.

Moving around, from place to place
My hands and feet stay in sacred space
Long may I flow and seek the truth
Let it go on till I merge with You

Song link: https://youtu.be/LxocPXl5zOw?si=k9uc12lIil4vBt65

5. Do I Need It?
This track expresses the spirit of *Aparigraha*, only taking what you need.

G
I know you've got stuff.
Houses, cars, clothes, gadgets and things
C   G
And you're looking for more, that's for sure.
      D
But do you have need, or is it
C   G
Just your sky-licking greed?

G
If you take too much.
Someone may go homeless, shirtless, toothless, luckless and more.
C   G
That's the way, the way the world works.
D   C   G
I think it's time to cut down on some of those perks.

     D   C
And before you grab anything, ask yourself one time,
G
Do I need it? Do I need it?

So, take what you need.
Get your food, clothes, medicine, shelter and all.
Take what you need, but nothing more.
You'll be happier than you ever were before

And before you grab anything, ask yourself one time,
Do I need it? Do I need it?

Song link: https://youtu.be/bW74Tw4FwHc?si=VPxDztfo106jTi3q

6. Squeaky Clean

This track speaks about the first item of *Niyama* practices which help us become pure and in harmony with our selves. It is the pursuit of *Shaocha*, cleanliness and purity of mind.

```
D              G         D
It's time to get so squeaky clean
                         A         D
Let your outside and inside shine like a beam.
A              G         D
Scrub your body clean your room
              A            G  D
You're gonna be glowing real soon.
```

Keep your mind peaceful and pure
Don't think about more, more, more.
Plant the seed of service in your soul
That's the way to be happy and whole

Bridge

```
G
Turn away from nasty sights
D
Smelly things, and screeching sounds.
G
Build a temple of love inside your heart
         A
It's time to make a fresh new start.
```

So be a friend to one and all
You'll be standing so straight and tall
Give whatever you can give
That's the way we all can live.

Song link: https://youtu.be/pnFY8oh2qZI?si=gILMSt_-ODqfFRyK

7. The Secret of It All
The yogic concept of Santosha, or contentment, is addressed by this song.
Capo on fret 2

```
G                        C
I did my work and I'm resting still
D              C         G
No need to chase for one more thrill
G                        C
I am happy as a dog wagging his tail.
D                    C    G
With a life like this how can I fail?

G                              Am
'Cause the secret of it all is to know when to stop
      C          G
and be content with whatever you've got.
```

I'm not gonna run after more and more
I've got some time to rest on the shore.
Some folks rush around like busy bees
They're never happy and never pleased.

'Cause the secret of it all is to know when to stop
and be content with what you've got.

So do your thing but remember to chill
You don't have to keep climbing that hill
No need to scramble near and far
Just take some time and gaze at the stars

'Cause the secret of it all is to know when to stop
and be content with what you've got.

Song links: https://youtu.be/gyxJh7Xb2RA?si=m4JjKBLFZ4_0OcfE

8. I Know I Must

Practicing penance to reach the goal is called *Tapah* and is another one of the Niyamas, practices that purify us. Penance here means service to others, taking the pains of others upon us.

Capo on fret 2 (optional)

```
G                         C        G
Let my karma burn away serving others every day
              D      G
Embers of my ego dim to dust.
G                    C     G
As I scrape away that age-old rust,
                    D      G
I'll shoulder your burden I know I must.
```

Everything that lives is just His form
There is no exception, it's the norm
I'm gonna serve all everywhere I go
And plunge my mind into the cosmic flow.

```
D                    G
I'll take your pain and make it mine
D                       G
I'll ease your load, and we will shine
D                             G
Be it a mountain, or a boulder or cosmic dust
D               C    G
I've got to serve all; I know I must.
```

It's time to stop thinking of me, me, me
I've got to open my heart and set it free.
I'll burst on through my mental crust
I've got to serve all; I know I must.

```
D                    G
I'll take your pain and make it mine
D                       G
I'll ease your load, and we will shine
D                             G
```

Be it a mountain, or a boulder or cosmic dust
D   C   G
I've got to serve all; I know I must.

Song link: https://youtu.be/SUK10qt0lq8?si=JYrN0P_ECpbPh8gq

9. Make it One With You

Svadhyaya, self-study, is another important pillar of yoga. This song expresses this endeavor to study and assimilate the wisdom of those who have gone before us.

G
If you need a bit of help when you hit the ground
Looking for some strength to turn it around
C
Listen to the words of those who walked before
G
Plunge into a good book and open the door.
D
You've got to catch the inner truth
C   G
And make it one with you.

Read it, remember it, and soak in all that's right
Embrace the eternal and expand your mind tonight
Merge your heart into to the cosmic flow,
Soar into the stars and let your love grow.

You've got to catch the inner truth
And make it one with you.

The ancient words of the noble ones
Dispel the darkness of the night.
Bathe your mind with the timeless truth
Catch the inner spirit and make it one with you.

You've got to catch the inner truth
And make it one with you

You can sit around the fire with some friendly souls
Listen to the stories as wisdom's bell tolls
Soak in the vibes of the wonderous night.
Throw yourself into the endless light.

You've got to catch the inner truth
And make it one with you.

You've got to catch the inner truth
And make it one with you.

https://youtu.be/n-x4o0A1TNc?si=oe1SP9dMsIdTREzX

10. The One True Love

Iishvara Pranidhana is the Sanskrit term for meditating on the goal. This is the last of the ethical pillars of yoga. It is meditation on the Supreme Consciousness, the goal of our life and the one true love!

Capo on fret 2

```
G
I'm going to my ultimate abode
I'm seeking to reach my one true home
    D             C
How long will it take till I rest my head
G
And cast away my heavy load?
           D         C      G
'Cause I'm meditating on the one true love
```

I'm bringing my mind to one point
Away from the tumult and noise
I'm watching it flow right into the light
gonna reach the realm of peace tonight
'Cause I'm meditating on the one true love

Flow on flow on flow on flow on
Flow on flow on flow on
The pulsing of my breath, the rhythms of my mind
Endless bliss beyond all space and time
'Cause I'm meditating on the one true love

```
Baba Nam Kevalam Baba Nam Kevalam
D                    C
Baba Nam Kevalam Baba Nam Kevalam
G
Baba Nam Kevalam
D                        C
Baba Nam Kevalam Baba Nam Kevalam
G
Baba Nam Kevalam
```

'Cause I'm meditating on the one true love

Song link: https://youtu.be/AfE70mFSo-o?si=NdTq3m3yk_llGGHr

I'm Just an Average Cosmic Being
Released May 16, 2022

1. I'm Just an Average Cosmic Being

This song started out as a challenge: my friend saw someone walking down the street wearing a button saying, "I'm Just An Average Cosmic Being." He asked me if I could write a country song with that title. So, I took up the challenge. In fact, we are all cosmic beings, with a common origin and a common destination. If we live up to our noble place in the universe, we will become great, even if we are "just average."

Capo 2 on the recorded version

D
Some folks put on airs
They say they just don't care
G
Others never think and
                    D
They'll quit you in a blink.
But me I'll never leave you
'Cause I know what you are feeling

    A   G   D
For I'm just an average Cosmic Being
    A   G   D
For I'm just an average Cosmic Being

You can shoot for the stars
Or steer your ship to Mars
But you'll have to keep on searching
To unravel life's real meaning.
But me I've got a plan
To find out what I can,

For I'm just an average Cosmic Being
For I'm just an average Cosmic Being

When all is said and done
Life's more than just a circus.
I hope that you'll agree that
we're living for a higher purpose
But me, I've made my mind up
To seek and never give up

For I'm just an average Cosmic Being
I'm just an average Cosmic being.
You can say I'm just an average Cosmic Being.

Song link: https://youtu.be/fZUXC8IpS5Q?si=eFus5-YZAteeZtQb

2. We Don't Need No Billionaires

Some years back the news media asked some would-be presidential candidates what their opinion about billionaires was. I was not candidate at the time. But if they had asked me my answer would be along the lines of this song.

Am
We don't need no billionaires,
G
Zillionaies or trillionaires,
F   E7
What we need is love, sweet love.
Am
How much does one person need?
G
I'm talking of need and not of greed
F   E7
I think there's just got to be a limit.

We're traveling together on a tiny green planet,
Let's make it work for everyone on it.
I think it's time to set the record straight.

Am
We don't need no billionaires,
G
Zillionaies or trillionaires,
F   E7
What we need is love, sweet love.

Am
We don't need your philanthropy
We're the human society.
We can decide what we need together.
We don't want you to buy our elections,
Make us follow your selections.
Our own choices will turn out so much better.

Chorus repeats: We don't need no…

Am
The billionaire over there saying
G
I create the wealth; I create the jobs
F
Without me you would all starve.
E7
Well, wait a minute mister,
Am
We're fixing your car, shining your shoes
G
Teaching your kids, growing your food.
F   E7
Building your plush little world.

Chorus: We don't need no.....

There's one more thing I've got to say,
Cooperation's the name of the game,
Selfish grabbing, oh, that's so lame, Mr. Billionaire.

Chorus: We don't need no...

Song link: https://youtu.be/-dD9x4AQz7M?si=2fk3IZ-GueSrb351

3. Get Ready It's Coming Your Way (lyrics by Alan Verdier and Dada Veda)
In June of 2021 a friend sent me an email with some text, a poem. He asked me to add music to it. The poem was in line with how I see the world, and I did it, changing only one small thing in the original text. The result is this song.
Capo on Fret 2

```
G         Em          Am        D
Wake up now from your deep, deep slumber.
G          Em      Am        D
The gloomy night is just about over.
     G    Em  Am        D
The new dawn brings a new day.
   C         D         G
Get ready it's coming your way.
```

Let's travel to eternity,
with all our minds in harmony.
We are part of the Cosmic Soul
like all in one and one in all.

```
Am
Melodies make a symphony
Em
as the rivers flow to the sea.
Am
We will merge with the universe
      D
in pure joy we will immerse.
```

The earth, the sea, the sky and stars
echo to my guitar
and in the corridors of time
we'll all dance Divine.

Wake up now from your deep, deep slumber.
The gloomy night is just about over.
The new dawn brings a new day.
Get ready it's coming your way.
Song link: https://youtu.be/_rURbgrmjDQ?si=aiBMGhCBbYRDAodM

4. Stay With Me Endlessly
This is a cosmic love song. The loved one can be God, or the person next to you. It is up to you.

```
D
When I look into your eyes
G         D
I can see the moon arise
D
When I gaze into your face
G         D
I fly across time and space
A         G
Stay with me endlessly
          D
We'll fly until eternity
```

Let's jump into the inner light
We'll chase the darkness of the night
We'll run beside a deep blue see
A gentle wind will set us free
Stay with me endlessly
We'll fly until eternity

We'll listen to a sound divine
We'll feel the bliss one more time
We'll gaze upon the setting sun
We'll share our joy with everyone
Stay with me endlessly
We'll fly until eternity

Song link: https://youtu.be/2Lfxl30IeM0?si=RYuC_eHGneInE-FP

5. We Don't Need No Corporations, Do We?
The corporation has been the main form of business organization for hundreds of years, but is it the best form that we can come up with? This song suggests that a cooperative model could give rights and dignity to all members as well as prosperity. As the lyrics state, you may not agree with this now, but one day you will.
Capo on fret 2

```
E
We don't need no Corporations, do we?
                          B7
We don't need no exploitation, do we?
E
We want out right to live and thrive
          A
Just as long as we're alive.
E            B7          E
We don't need no corporations, do we?
```

I can vote for the president but not the boss.
That's not democracy and that's my loss.
Here's something better you'll one day agree
Let's run everything cooperatively.

Let the workers in a place guide their fate,
give them a voice, give them a stake
They'll become the owners, and managers too
Prosperity will flow to me and you.

We don't need no corporations, do we?
We Don't need no exploitation, do we?
We want out right to live and thrive
Just as long as we're alive.
We don't need no corporations, do we?

It's time to kick the traders from the temple, let's do it
Let's bid farewell to the wheeler-dealers, let's do it
Let's watch the tide of cooperation
Open the door to our liberation.
We don't need no corporations, do we?

Song link: https://youtu.be/M0OiX8UZlPE?si=Y34c1GuZnG41-9Tu

6. Hope on the Horizon

I went for my daily walk through the forest, and the phrase "hope on the horizon" popped into my head. I started singing any old tune to that phrase. Later, I worked on the lyrics and refined the melody, and this song is the result. The near future could be problematic, but I am sure that there truly is hope on the horizon for humanity.

Capo on Fret 2

G
When I look around at the good things to be found
Then I understand that we are glory bound, and
C   G
There is hope on the horizon, hope on the horizon
D   C
Hope on the Horizon, hope on the horizon
G
Hope on the Horizon for humanity

G
Feel the morning sunshine, catch a gentle breeze
Listen to the children singing pretty melodies
          C
And you'll hear hope on the horizon,
G   D
Hope on the Horizon, hope on the horizon
C   G
Hope on the Horizon, hope on the horizon for you and me

Whatever comes before us, together we will face
You know we've got the strength of the entire human race
And there's hope on the horizon, hope on the horizon
Hope on the Horizon, hope on the horizon

Hope on the Horizon for humanity

So, lend a helping hand, pitch in what you can
We're gonna show the world that we've got a plan
And there's hope on the horizon, hope on the horizon
Hope on the Horizon, hope on the horizon
Hope on the Horizon for humanity

Song link: https://youtu.be/XbtrxuTY1jE?si=cEsyJoHTgSz-60fs

7. You've Got to Move On
I heard a story about Rohit a great scholar in Vedic times who was lethargic. His father, a manual laborer, scolded him. His father said "when a person's face get perspired due to constant labor, the beauty of the face of that person is unprecedented. Since that is the perspiration due to hard labor, its beauty is flawless and unparalleled. Even Indra, the king of gods aspires for befriending such a person."
Capo on Fret 4

Am
When you lie a lump
Your fate lies sleeping
G
Get up and move on and stop the weeping
F
Sit up and get up your fate will awake
E7   Am
Move on, move on let's make the word shake.

With the sweat on your brow like diamonds on a crown
You've got to move on, you've got to move on
Leave the dark age behind, hold your fate in your hand
Move on, move on, it's time to make your stand.

No need to check the stars or look in a mirror,
Your future is bright, your future is bright
Get up and move on, let's set things right.
We're gonna change the world, let's start it tonight.

Song link: https://youtu.be/CL72VxbpfnU?si=lbUfwq1APqE71t1Q

8. Everybody Hates Capitalism

This is based on a true story. I was showing a young friend some social media projects I work on, including a podcast with the sub-title "Moving Beyond Capitalism." My friend looked at it and casually said, "Yeah, everybody hates capitalism." And that sparked this song.

Capo on fret 4 in the recorded version

Am
I was talking to a young friend the other day
G
About the world and where it's heading.
F
He looked all around at the things going down,
E7
he turned to me and then he said, he said:

Am
"Everybody hates capitalism
G
Everybody hates exploitation
Am
Everybody loves cooperation
G   Am
Let's put an end to this frustration now"

Anything more bothering you?

He said:

"We're working like slaves for corporate owners
Never knowing when our time is up,
We're thrown out of work when a glitch hits the system
And then we become innocent victims."

Tell me more!

"No one likes to see children starving,
No one likes to hear a bully boasting
No one likes to see the good crushed

No one likes their voices being hushed, oh yeah

A few get rich and move ahead
Yet millions stagnate, nearly dead
Some places get splendid amenities
Others lack basic facilities, yeah

Private wealth is glorified,
But public needs are crucified
Corruption and elitism rule the land
Kindness and wisdom are buried in the sand."

That's why

"Everybody hates capitalism
Everybody hates exploitation
Everybody loves cooperation
Let's put an end to this frustration."

Well, what are you going to do about it.

"We're gonna replace it sooner or later
With something fairer, something greater
We're all fed up with the same old, same old.
We need something new, something bold
Let's build a world for our children's, children
It's time to liberate the earth's billions."

And just in case your forgot:

Everybody hates capitalism
Everybody hates exploitation
Everybody loves cooperation
Let's put an end to this frustration, now!"

Song link: https://youtu.be/FhOkUfgNJeo?si=QsGt48SdGAmkwCxP

9. Float on the Wave of Bliss

This is a mystical song. Yoga philosophy says that this world of diverse forms originates from one blissful formless source. Through a process of evolution and struggle the diverse forms progress and move on to finally merge with the One. This simple song tries to capture this immense concept. "One becomes many, and many become one."

```
D                                  Em
It's a strange, strange world that we live in
A               G          D
One becomes many and many become one

D                                  Em
It's a dance of Shiva and Shakti
A               G          D
weaving the fabric of the world
D
Unravel the thread, unravel the mystery
Em         A7.          D
Become one with the weaver
D
Unravel the thread, unravel the mystery
Em             A7.       D
And float on the waves of bliss.
Em             A7       D
Float on the waves of bliss

Em                          Bm
 'cause we're moving along through time and space
Em                 Bm
Not sure where we are going
Em                 Bm
We're moving along from place to place
Em                  A7
As the river of life keeps flowing
```

This great big world is a sound stage
many sounds becoming one
listen to the sound, merge in the sound
float on the waves of bliss

listen to the sound, merge in the sound
float on the waves of bliss

listen to the sound, merge in the sound
float on the waves of bliss
float on the waves of bliss

Solo Section: Same chords as verse 1

Verse 1 is repeated after the solo.

Song link: https://youtu.be/OxI2RWJKwXs?si=kSCCyi7ITyBPTSxR

10. Baba Nam Kevalam

This is a mantra music track, also known as kirtan or kiirtan. Baba Nam Kevalam is a mantra with the meaning "Only the name of the most beloved" sometimes translated as "love is all there is"

Capo 2 optional, the recorded version uses it

G   D
Baba Nam Kevalam
Em   C
Baba Nam Kevalam
G   D   G
Baba Nam Kevalam

Repeat first section

C   D   G
Baba Nam Kevalam repeat this line four times

Song link: https://youtu.be/GcE43GeIEMg?si=PdWf1UCRH4U0tnjX

Bring About a Better Day
released August 12, 2024

This is the ninth studio album by Dada Veda. It was primarily recorded in Urbana, IL with remote contributions from artists in Michigan, New Jersey and Sweden. Seven of the songs are original compositions of Dada Veda and four are songs in the Prabhat Samgiita collection written by P.R. Sarkar. The last track is a kirtan devotional chant using the Baba Nam Kevalam mantra.

1. Bring About a Better Day

Em7
God don't care what color skin you have
Am7
And God don't care how you pray
Em7
God don't care what passport you carry
Am7   D
and God don't care where you stay

C   D
All God knows is your pure, pure soul
C   D
He wants to see you happy and whole
C   D
To serve all beings come what may
C   D   G
And bring about a better day.

God don't care where you're from
and God don't care what you own
God don't care what you're wearing
And God don't care if you're well known.

All God knows is your pure, pure soul
He wants to see you happy and whole
To serve all beings come what may
And bring about a better day.

God don't care who you follow
God don't care what you read
And God don't care just what you believe now
Cause God don't belong to any creed.

All God knows is your pure, pure soul
He wants to see you happy and whole
To serve all beings come what may
And bring about a better day

Song link: https://youtu.be/vxdH2-4zFgo?si=ow7OLCJpBLO1vKWJ

2. We are Never Alone or Helpless

This is a new recording of this song which originally appeared on my second album, done with a lot of help from my friends in Sweden as well as vocal backing from Michigan.

G
When the problems of the world lay heavy in your head,
  C   G
And you don't know where to turn.
Why don't you go inside and find your inner strength
D   C   G
And remember a lesson we must learn.
G
We are never alone or helpless.
 C   G
The force that guides the stars guides us too.
We are never alone or helpless
D   C   G
The force that guides the stars guides us too.

G
When you're down and out and feeling kind of low,
C   G
Don't give up the fight.
G
Because there's one more thing
I think that you should know.
D   C D
You're guided by an inner light.

We are never alone or helpless.
The force that guides the stars guides us too.
We are never alone or helpless
The force that guides the stars guides us too.

So start each day with a bouncing stride,
And finish it with a smile.
And if you should ever lose your way,
Remember He's with us all the while

Song link https://www.youtube.com/watch?v=Yo-ow69S0TM

3. Crimson Dawn

A song about the coming of humanity's bright future. This is a new recording of the song which originally appeared on the first album.

```
  E              A
I'm waiting for a new day's light,
              B7        E
I 'm hoping for a future that's bright.
  E                       A
I'm watching a new world being born,
              B7        E
Soon I'm gonna see a crimson dawn.
```

This world is big enough for all,
It's just that our minds are too small,
To see the beauty of all things,
And the happiness that harmony brings.

I'm waiting for a new day's light,
I 'm hoping for a future that's bright.
I'm watching a new world being born,
Soon I'm gonna see a crimson dawn.

I think it's time to live and let live,
Stop grabbing, start learning how to give.
How long will it take for us to know,
That the secret of life is letting go?

I'm waiting for a new day's light,
I 'm hoping for a future that's bright.
I'm watching a new world being born,
Soon I'm gonna see a crimson dawn.

Song Link: https://www.youtube.com/watch?v=pPlvSSmlvXc

4. Lend the World Your Helping Hand
A song based on P.R. Sarkar's message reminding us to be great by our actions that will help the world rather than by rhetoric.

D
It is action that makes a person great
G   D
Tall talks are useless.

When you do something good don't you hesitate
G   A   D
Get started before it's too late.

D
Be great by your spiritual work,
G   D
Be great by your service.
D
Be great your sacrifice,
G   A   D
Lend the world your helping hand.

Pretty words can never feed a man
Though they may look good on paper
Roll up your sleeves and give a hand.
Do whatever you can.

Be great by your spiritual work,
Be great by your service.
Be great your sacrifice,
Lend the world your helping hand.

There is still some time to make things right
Though the picture does look hopeless.
Kick out the jams, let's start tonight.
We're gonna build a world that's safe and bright.

Be great by your spiritual work,
Be great by your service.

Be great your sacrifice,
Lend the world your helping hand.

Song link: https://www.youtube.com/watch?v=sPUK7fQ--m4

5. Back to You The Reincarnation Song

Someone asked me if I could write a song on this topic. It is not really possible to explain it fully in a small song, but I did my best to express what I think is the gist.

```
C
I tumbled through space
G
in deep, deep sleep
F            C
Ready to try on another me.
F            G          C   F G
About to resume my journey back to You.

C         G
Born again, struggling to know
F             C
What's going on in this latest show.
F         G          C   FG
All the while restless to be with You.

F
Getting closer to the end
C
I feel You more and more.
F
My mind becomes lost in love,
G
Look I'm flying high above!
```

No rebirth, nothing to repeat
At last this trip is now complete
Glad that I finally made it back to You.
By your grace I made it back to You.

Song link: https://youtu.be/uJWU44xxO2o?si=Hm1ARkNn31f1DCzu

6. Just Beyond Your Mind

This song is based on imagery in poems by the mystical poet Kabir 1440-1518 who observed that people chase for various kinds of wealth neglecting the tremendous wealth lying at the core of their beings.

```
  D       G       A           D
I wandered around thirsty for a drink
                  G         A         D
Like a mad man crying in the desert heat
         G         A        D
I never saw the water around me
            G     A      D
'Til one day I listened to the breeze.
```

```
            G      A              D
It said, "stop, look, wake up from your sleep
                G     A          D
whatever you seek is closer than you think
              G     A       D
Plunge within and surely you will find
              G     A        D
A soothing source just beyond your mind."
```

I was trying to find a garden of bright flowers
Traveling here and there for countless hours
but I never saw that garden deep within
Til one day I listened to the breeze.

It said, "stop, look, wake up from your sleep
whatever you seek is closer than you think
Plunge within and surely you will find
A soothing source just beyond your mind."

Now I know that it's right inside of me
Like a sprout lying hidden deep within a seed
And should I ever lose my way
I will take some time and listen to the breeze

Saying "stop, look, wake up from your sleep

whatever you seek is closer than you think
Plunge within and surely you will find
A soothing source just beyond your mind."

Song link: https://youtu.be/hAzoG-NWLdY?si=-_ZGrWAoyjL5CQV8

7. Humanity's Call

This is the first song that I ever wrote, back in 2002. The recording was never done until 2024. Thematically it sets the stage for all my songs, calling for an awakening of consciousness in the world.

```
G            Em        C      D
Wake up my friend, step into the sun
         G          Em     C D G
Let's move together to a distant shore.
G             Em      C   D
Where love and bliss reign supreme.
G        Em        C   D G
Hurry my friend let's wait no more.
```

We stumbled in darkness for endless days
Hurting each other for no reason at all.
Now is the time to change our ways,
Tuning ourselves to Humanity's call.

C
Look at the pain and give your love
G
It's not too late to start a new game.
C
Let's turn those frowns right into smiles.
D
Hurry my friend, let's catch that train.

We were separate for so many lonely days.
Split by miles of towering walls.
Now is the time to change our ways,
Tuning ourselves to Humanity's call.

Song link: https://youtu.be/jIe24ZBLSH8?si=16rE3mxWuWR0Zl9j

8. Sakal Maner Viina

This is the fourth song in the Prabhat Samgiita catalog of PR Sarkar. It is also called the Song of Sweetness. It is in the Bengali language.
Capo on fret 2

```
D                            G              D
Sa'kal maner viiná ek sure báje áj, Sa'kal hrdaye saorabh 2x
D             G         A
Nandana madhusáje ele tumi dhará májhe 2x
D      A      D
Dile sabe ek anubhav 2x
```

Sa'kal maner viiná ek sure báje áj, Sa'kal hrdaye saorabh 2x
Chiṋro ná chiṋro ná e kusuma málákháni 2x
Mamatár sárá vaebhav 2x

Sa'kal maner viiná ek sure báje áj, Sa'kal hrdaye saorabh 2x
Eśo tumi áro káche, áro káche, áro káche 2x
Niye jáo jáhá kichu sab 2x

Sa'kal maner viiná ek sure báje áj, Sa'kal hrdaye saorabh 2x

The lute of every mind is playing the same tune today
In every heart there is a sweet fragrance.
In sweet garb my Beloved appeared in the midst of the world,
Giving all one feeling.
Do not tear, do not tear my flower-garland,
My entire supply of loving feelings.
Come closer, closer, and still closer please,
Take all that I have.

Song link: https://youtu.be/aE4Ufu2WR2c?si=u06CUV5tuFIXDPom

9. Ajana Pathik

This is song number 1698 in the Prabhat Samgiita collection of songs written by spiritual teacher P.R. Sarkar Anandamurti. Ajana Pathik means the "unknown traveler" and it refers to God.

```
Em          D         Em
```
Ajaná pathik, thámo go kśańik 2x
```
D             Em
```
Tomáy parábo málá
```
Em          D         Em
```
Kusum paráge smita anuráge 2x
```
Em
```
Sájáye enechi d́álá
```
D             Em
```
Tomáy parábo málá

Ajáná pathik, thámo go kśańik 2x
tomáy parábo málá

```
Em              D
```
Gán geye caliyáchi tomáre tuśite
```
Em              D         Em
```
Sure laye sádhiyáchi tava saḿgiite
```
Em          D         Em
```
Priiti saḿvite madhumákhá cite 2x
```
D             Em
```
Mandrita man mekhalá
```
D             Em
```
Tomáy parábo málá

Ajáná pathik, thámo go kśańik 2x
tomáy parábo málá

Chande chande náci tomáre barite
Ucchal ánande sudhár sarite
Cái ná kichu nite cái shudhu dite 2x
Bhálobásá paráń d́hála´
Tomáy parábo málá

O unknown traveler,
please wait a moment.
So I can garland you.

I have decorated with smiles and affection a
fragrant floral basket.
So I can garland you.

I have continued to sing songs for You.
I am trying to be in tune with Your melody.
My restless mind wants to be tied to
Your loving, honey-like sweetness.
I want to garland you.

I dance in rhythm to attract You
In the changing world,
flowing in the stream of nectar.
I don't want to take anything,
I only want to give.
Just to pour out my love to you.

I want to garland you.

Song link: https://youtu.be/yCUgCjrUaEg?si=mE5Tr6eaz2lq5nJp

10. Nayan Majhare

This is song number 1315 in the Prabhat Samgiita collection of songs written by P.R. Sarkar Anandamurti

```
D                    G
Tumi nayan majhare rayecho ta'i
A      G        D
Nayan parena dekhite
D         A          G
Nija rupete perecho lukote

D              G    D
Tumi vira't' purus' an'u je savi,
D          G      D
Tava a'shray sakale labhi
D            G      D
Tava karuna'y tava prerana'y
A        G      D
Toma'ri pathe pari calite
D       A          G
Nija rupete perecho lukote

D           G     D
Tumi a'cho dev amita ka'ler,
D         G     D
Sapta loker ameya baler
D         G      D
He priyatama nikatatama
A              G    A  D
Ghare va'hire theko sukhe dukhete
```

You are in the midst of my eyes,
That's why my eyes cannot see You.
You have hidden Yourself in Your own form.
You are great and everything is within you,

Everyone takes shelter in You.
By your grace and by Your compassion,
Let me continue to move towards You.

Oh Lord, you exist for eternal time in the seven realms,
There is no power but You.
Oh nearest and dearest one,
You remain with me always, in pleasure and pain.

Song link: https://youtu.be/AnH0muaf6zE?si=4c7L1tmYsswfgTU0

11. Anek Shuniya

This is song number 1041 in the Prabhat Samgiita song collection by P.R. Sarkar Anandamurti

```
D         G      D
Anek shuniya' anek bha'viya',
          A        D
Toma'kei bha'lobesechi
D              G        D
A'ka'sh pa'ta'l girl kandare ghure
D    A     D
Ratna eki peyechi.
'
D              G        A
Ja'ni bha'loba'sa' na'hi ma'ne yukti,
               G   A D
Bha'lobese a'mi na'hi ca'hi mukti.
                       G      A
A'mi bha'loba'si a'nanda pa'va'ra la'gi,
D    A   D
E katha'i sa'r jenechi.
```

Tava ka'j kare ya'vo yatha'shakti,
Mane rekhe sav sera' para'bhakti.
A'mi bha'loba'si a'nanda deva'ra la'gi,
E kotha'i shes' vujhechi.

I heard so much about You and I thought much about You; then I learned to love You.

I searched for You In the sky, on the earth, and in the mountain caves

I finally I found a unique jewel in my life.
I know that love does not obey any logic
By love I don't want liberation
I only love You to get Your bliss.
This Is the essence that I've come to understand.

I will go on doing Your work with sincere effort,
keeping the Supreme devotion In my mind.
I love You to make You happy.
This Is the ultimate thing that I have realized.

Song link: https://youtu.be/5RqqTUHz3K0?si=XDa3Sk4y8subuvzQ

12. Baba Nam Kevalam 2024

Baba Nam Kevalam is a Sanskrit mantra which means "Only the name of the most beloved". That "most beloved" is God and a common understanding of the mantra is that "Love is all there is." This is. a good song to sing before meditation and the mantra can also be used in silent meditation. Try it!

```
D            G        A
Baba Nam Kevalam Baba Nam Kevalam
D            G        A
Baba Nam Kevalam Baba Nam Kevalam
G            A        D
Baba Nam Kevalam Baba Nam Kevalam
G            A        D
Baba Nam Kevalam Baba Nam Kevalam
```

Song link: https://youtu.be/zfAeDeNSo_4?si=eG-wWQsNF6_lxUd5

Carry Me Along
released October 1, 2025

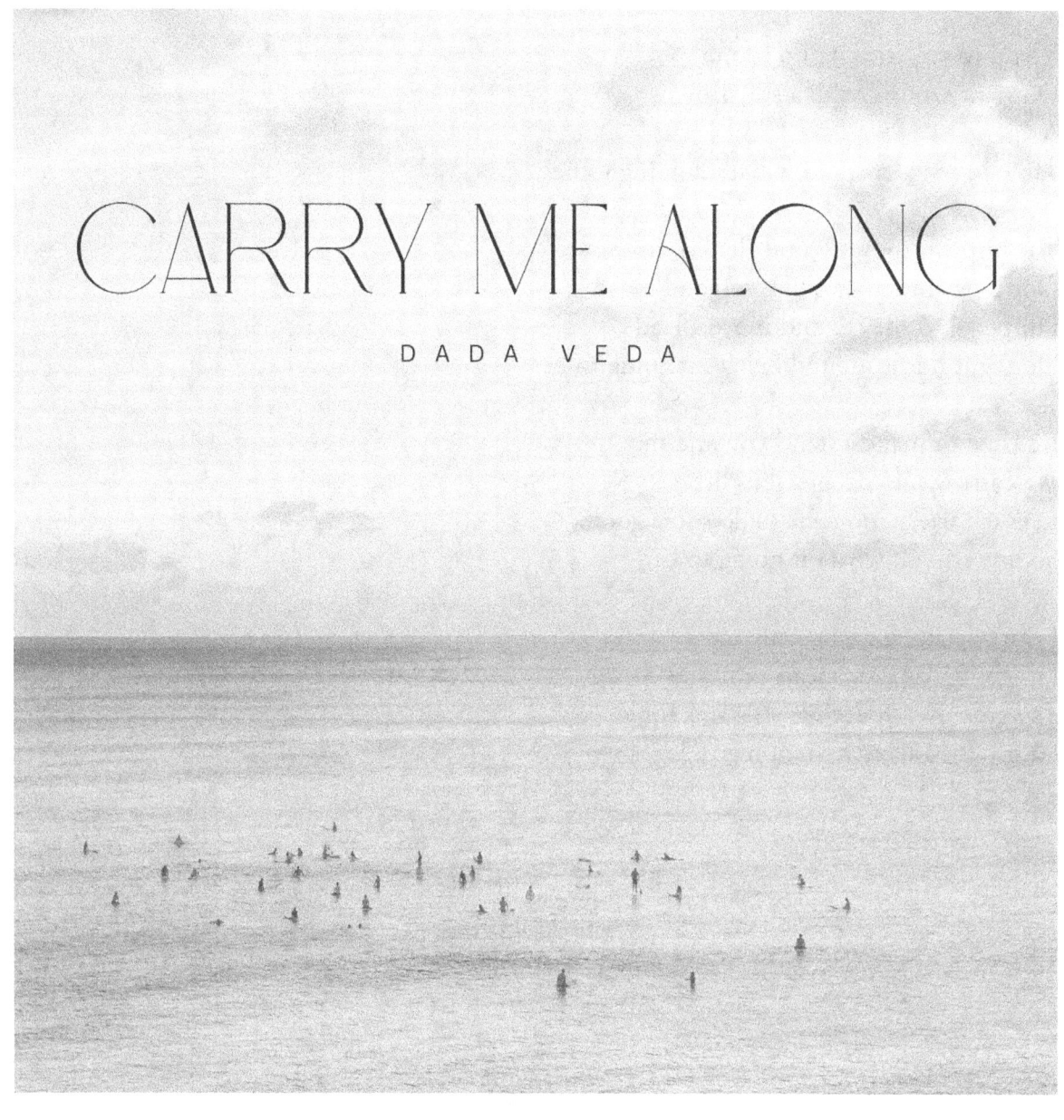

1. What's it Going to Be?
According to some philosophers, only human beings have a chance to decide whether they are to accelerate their progress or even regress on the evolutionary journey. This song poses this choice to us.

```
E
We can go up or we can go down.
      A           E
It's up to you and it's up to me
Don't sit around with a silly frown.
A                     B7           E
Time to make a choice what's it going to be?
```

The birds in the trees and the fish in the sea
Don't get this chance like you and me
Put pedal to the gas and move ahead
Don't hit fiddle around, what's it going to be?

It's time to make a stand you and me
We can't waste this precious life.
Let's use every moment to do some good.
So, my friend, what's it going to be?

I can't decide for you, only me
I'm going to push ahead earnestly
Towards the One while sing this song
So my friend, what's it going to be?

Song link: https://dadaveda.bandcamp.com/track/whats-it-going-to-be

2. Been There, Done That

After years of incessant travel, I have slowed down and am relatively stationary. This song explains my observations of this voyage.

```
G         C           G
I traveled across the world
         C      G
Seen a lot of scenes
            C         G
Went to the ends of the earth
C        D     G
Taking in everything.
```

Some people I saw were poor
Others living so high.
Everybody running around
Nobody wanted to cry.

```
G       Em      D       C         G
But when it comes down to what really counts
        Em    D       C     G
You'll finally see that it's you and me
Em      D     C       G
Trying to make sense of it all.
Em      D     C        G
Trying to reach our inner soul.
```

So when you ask me to go here
You ask me to go there.
All that I can say is that I've been there and done that
I've been there and done that.

Song link: https://dadaveda.bandcamp.com/track/been-there-done-that

3. Guide Me to Unending Bliss

I first started writing this song in 2004 on some handwritten notes. I kept the manuscript and finished it 21 years later. At first, I was not sure what I was writing, but it turned out to be a prayer for guidance.

```
G                           C
Golden friend in the awakening sunlight
G                           D
Embrace my soul and hold me tight
G                           C
Fill my mind with the peace of morning
G        D        G
Carry me beyond the reach of Night
```

Wipe the dust from my darkest corners
Flood my heart with the call of love
Bathe me in the morning sunshine
Show me the wonder in the sky above.

```
D                           G
I'll plunge inside your pool of kindness
        D                   G
And fix my gaze on your beam of light.
D                           G
I'll throw my arms wide around you
        D                   G
And move to a realm oh so bright.
```

Take me across the sea of sorrow
Lead the way to a brilliant tomorrow
Help me pierce the cloud of darkness
Guide me to Unending bliss
Guide me to Unending bliss
Guide me to Unending bliss.
Song link: https://dadaveda.bandcamp.com/track/guide-me-to-unending-bliss

4. It's Time to Turn Things Around

Within each of us there is the potential to do something great, that's why whenever we get in a "down" mood we should remember this and turn our present condition around.

```
G
Do you know who you are?
Em
Are you chasing near and far,
Am                      G
Are you waiting for life to begin?
                        Em
Are you lost and alone and afraid of the unknown?
Am        D       G
Not sure where you can fit in?

G                       Em
Does it seem like your life has passed you by
          Am          G
And you're living from day to day.
                        Em
Then stop for a while and clear your mind
       Am      D       G
and listen to what I have to say

C
Take another look at what you can do
G
Go explore that inner you
              C
You'll will the find the strength and your real true worth
       D         G
It's there inside of you
```

So don't be afraid don't be unsure
When the Love Supreme is with you.
Go boldly in this world turn it upside down
It's time to turn things around

Song link: https://dadaveda.bandcamp.com/track/its-time-to-turn-things-around

5. We've Just Got to Hang On

This song addresses the age-old question of how we can
have so much evil and chaos in a world created by an all-knowing Supreme Being.

```
G                              C
They say that God is good, and that God is great
            D       G
Yet this world is full of hate.
                    C
How can this be I want to know
D               G
Tell me before it's too late
```

Some say it's just a show, a cosmic play
A production from the one above
Heroes and villains are fighting it out.
And we've just got to hang on

```
C
If you came in act two and you missed act one
G
You're never gonna know the score
            C
But if you stick around for the whole darn thing.
        D
You'll jump and cheer for more.
```

Cause it's a tale that'll show us what to do
and what we've got to shun
It's got a lot more thrills than a fairy tale.
So we've just got to hang on

Song link: https://dadaveda.bandcamp.com/track/weve-just-got-to-hang-on

6. I Wish I Had an Orchestra

Sometimes it is said that one song can influence millions and change the world. I wish I had the tools to write and sing this song.

```
D                       G          D
I wish I had an orchestra, a great choir too
    G                   D
To play the sounds that will change the world
    A                   D
And make all our dreams come true.
```

The music will sing a tale
Of what we can achieve
So many voices moving in time
Sounding an anthem of peace.

This may sound like a crazy dream but
it's what I wish to see
Where every child can look ahead
To a bright destiny

```
    G
So let our song ring loud and clear
    D
We want to live as one.
G
Underneath that bright blue sky
      A
One day it will be done.
```

Repeat first verse

Song link: https://dadaveda.bandcamp.com/track/i-wish-i-had-an-orchestra

7. Behind the Many (All is One)

We live in a world of great diversity but behind the diversity there is one supreme consciousness. I tried to express this idea in this song.
Capo on fret 1

```
Em
One great soul shines in everyone
D                                Em
Sparkling and reflecting in different minds
Em
Tangled in knots that cannot be undone
D                   Em
Behind the many all is one.


C G D Em  C D Em

I can see the reflections from the sun on high
In countless streams and ponds below
Endless objects dance through my eyes
Behind the many all is one

C          D            G
I can see it in a baby's twinkling eyes
C           G       D
In the nod of the passers by
C              D        G
In the mountain's cold blue ice
            Am                      Em
Coloring the clouds of our great blue sky
```

One great soul shines in everyone
Sparkling and reflecting in different minds
Tangled in knots that cannot be undone
Behind the many all is one.
Song link: https://dadaveda.bandcamp.com/track/behind-the-many-all-is-one

8. I'm Moving to Perfection
The fundamental distinguishing characteristic (Dharma) of human beings is that we can move towards perfection. I celebrate this idea in this song.

```
D
I'm moving to perfection
Hoping to be on my way
G
I'm moving to perfection
                    D
Don't want any delay.
        A
Gonna expand my mind
G           D
Dip in the cosmic flow
        A
Gonna expand my mind and
G               D
Merge with the cosmic soul.
```

I'm serving the world
Because that's the thing to do
I'm serving world
Gonna make everything brand-new
Gonna carry the woes of me and you
Gonna dash the clouds and watch the sky turn blue.

I'm merging my mind, merging with the cosmic soul
I'm merging my heart gonna make my existence whole
That's what human life is all about
That's why I've come here to sing and shout.

I'm moving to perfection
Hoping to be on my way
I'm moving to perfection
Don't want any delay.
Gonna expand my mind
Dip in the cosmic flow
Gonna expand my heart and

Merge with the cosmic soul.

Song link: https://dadaveda.bandcamp.com/track/im-moving-to-perfection

9. Enough of This, Enough of That

We have too much hate in today's world. This song will hopefully make us aware and correct it.

```
D              A
Enough of this, enough of that
Bm                     G
Enough of hate for our fellow man
G     D               Bm
There is more than enough to go around
              G       A
And we don't want it in our town.

             D             A
We're all just passing through this show
      Bm              G
We're immigrants for all we know.
             D         A
Here for a while, then we're gone
             G         A  D
Hardly enough time to even sing this song.

D                   A
What's so hard about living together
Bm                  G
Sharing like sages of the past
D                   A
What's so hard about live and let live
G                   A
```

I think we can do it at last.
Bm   G
We all want to live, but we all have to give
F#m   E
I know that's the way to work this out
D   A
So, enough of this and enough of that
Bm   G   D
Enough of this hate for our fellow man.

Song link: https://dadaveda.bandcamp.com/track/enough-of-this-enough-of-that

11. Guide Me Lord

This is a basic prayer.

Am
Guide me lord and take this food
G
I offer it all to Thee
F
Take my body, it is yours
      E7
For as long as it will be.
      Am
Guide me Lord

Guide me along this path so bright
Show me what do
Help me to the serve this world with light
I leave it up to You.
Guide me Lord

G
Let me make somebody smile
F
If it only be a while
G
I want to make the most of this chance
F   E7
To see the world sing and dance.
      Am
Guide me Lord

Guide me Lord and hear this song
I'm singing it to you
Let it ring out in all the world
In a tune that sure and true.

Song link: https://dadaveda.bandcamp.com/track/guide-me-lord

12. Carry Me Along

In 2014 I wrote an autobiographical memoir (From Brooklyn to Benares and Back) talking about my life. Here I tell the same story in a short song.

G
I did so many crazy deeds,
D
Had so many zany thoughts
    G   C
With a restless mind I marched along
D   G
Searching through the weeds.

I searched high and low
For what I did not know.
Yet things finally turned out right
As I followed a Cosmic glow.

It's something I never believed
It's something I couldn't conceive,
How a divine call would guide me on
To my life's destiny.

So carry me along
with your enchanting song
take my life and make it strong
For all eternity.

Carry me along
with your enchanting song
take my life and make it strong
For all eternity

Baba Nam Kevalam
Baba Nam Kevalam
Baba Nam Kevalam
Baba Nam Kevalam

Song link: https://dadaveda.bandcamp.com/track/carry-me-along

Kiirtan (Mantra Chanting) Tutorials

This section is a guide to video tutorials in which I show how to play the Baba Nam Kevalam mantra using simple guitar chords. The mantra literally translates as "Only the name of the most beloved" and a common version of this is "Love is all there is." The chords are shown here and use the tutorial link to see the video showing the melody and the method of playing the songs.

Tutorial Number 1

(Capo on fret 2)

```
Em.         D   Em        D   Em
Baba Nam Kevalam, Baba Nam Kevalam. (2x)
Em          D   Em
Baba Nam Kevalam,
D           Em
Baba Nam Kevalam
```

Strum pattern: Down Down Up Down Up Down Up (DDUDUDU)

Tutorial link: https://www.youtube.com/watch?v=8JhTL4G1rbA&t=2s

Tutorial Number 2

```
D       A D   D      A D
Baba Nam Kevalam Baba Nam Kevalam
A       G A D A      G A D
Baba Nam Kevalam Baba Nam Kevalam
D   G       D   D   G       D
Baba Nam Kevalam Baba Nam Kevalam
```

Strum pattern: Down Down Up Down Up Down Up (DDUDUDU)

Tutorial link: https://www.youtube.com/watch?v=ns7ap684A8s&t=94s

Tutorial Number 3

```
Em      C    D        Em
Baba Nam Kevalam Baba Nam Kevalam   (2x)
Em  D Em    D Em  Em  D Em     D
Baba Nam  Kevalam    Baba Nam  Kevalam
```

Tutorial link: https://www.youtube.com/watch?v=1vYWNkHLMAQ

Tutorial Number 4

```
Em            C    D         Em
Baba Nam Kevalam Baba Nam Kevalam. (2x)
Em         C      D          Em
Baba Nam Kevalam Baba Nam Kevalam
```

The strumming pattern used is Down, Down, Up Down Up Down Up

Tutorial Number 5 (Bandhu He Tune)

```
D        A   D   D       A   D
Baba Nam Kevalam Baba Nam Kevalam (2x)
A          G       D
Baba Nam Kevalam Baba Nam Kevalm
```

Tutorial link: https://www.youtube.com/watch?v=kaMNiKUvqEg

Tutorial No. 6

```
Em      C   G   D    C       GD
Baba Nam Kevalam Baba Nam Kevalam
Em         C     D         G
Baba Nam Kevalam Baba Nam Kevalam
```

Tutorial link: https://www.youtube.com/watch?v=xJG0BMcERxE&t=123s

Tutorial No. 7

Capo on fret 3

```
G        C         G          D
Baba Nam Kevalam Baba Nam Kevalam (2x)
     Em       C         G          D
Baba Nam Kevalam Baba Nam Kevalam (2x)
```

Tutorial link: https://www.youtube.com/watch?v=ge7DkNjBRJU&t=17s

Tutorial No. 8

Capo on fret 3

```
C        G        F         C
Baba Nam Kevalam Baba Nam Kevalam (2x)
     Am           G
Baba Nam Kevalam Baba Nam Kevalam
       F             C
Baba Nam Kevalam Baba Nam Kevalam
```

Tutorial link: https://www.youtube.com/watch?v=ge7DkNjBRJU&t=17s

Tutorial No. 9

```
D       G  D        A   D
Baba Nam Kevalam Baba Nam Kevalam (2x)
G A D   G A D  G A D    G A D
Baba Nam Kevalam Baba Nam Kevalam
```

Tutorial link: https://www.youtube.com/watch?v=bLtwJqUxlyo

Appendix

Guitar Chord Chart

Here are the chords you will need for all the songs in this book. Most of them are open chords but there are a few barre chords too.

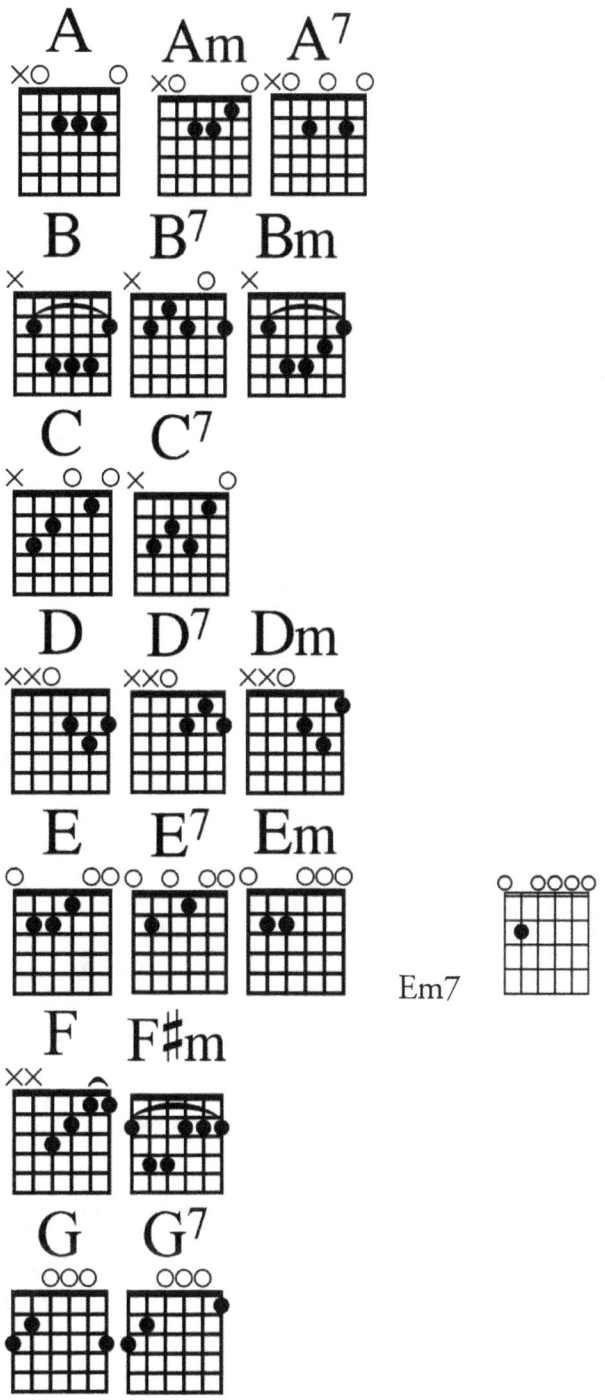

Song Index

A Better Deal	24
Ajana Pathik	132
Anek Shuniya	136
As the Word Spins Around	11
As the World Spins Around	30
Baba Nam Kevalam	118
Baba Nam Kevalam 2024	138
Baba Nam Kevalam	72
Back to You The Reincarnation Song	127
Been There, Done That	141
Behind the Many (All is One)	146
Be Kind to Everyone	84
Be Kind to Everyone	88
Better Than That	65
Brighter Than the Sun	4
Bring About a Better Day	120
Carry Me Along	151
Clouds Are Floating	53
Common Home	5
Crazy Bliss	85
Crazy Old Town	81
Crimson Dawn	10
Crimson Dawn	124
Do I Need it?	83
Do I Need It?	93
Don't Take It	77
Don't Take It	90
Do What You Can (written by Dada Veda)	48
Drift in Bliss	69
Enough of This, Enough of That	148
Everybody Hates Capitalism	114
Float on the Wave of Bliss	116
Forever and Ever	16
For Everyone	6
From Zero to Hero	19
Get Ready It's Coming Your Way (lyrics by Alan Verdier and Dada Veda)	108
Good Morning Dear Earth, Good Morning Dear Sun (public domain)	56
Good Old Kiirtan Baba Nam Kevalam	28

Guide Me Lord	150
Guide Me to Unending Bliss	142
Hope on the Horizon	112
Humanity's Call	130
I Can Never Be Apart From You	9
I Don't Eat Meat	12
I Know I Must	96
I Know You Can't Be Far	22
In the Stillness of the Morning	8
I See Your Smile	71
I See Your Smile	92
It Takes a Caring Heart	75
It's the System	38
It's Time to Turn Things Around	143
I Wish I Had an Orchestra	145
I'd Really Like to Know	42
I'm Just an Average Cosmic Being	104
I'm Moving to Perfection	147
I'm Waiting for that Time	23
Just Being Good, Is Not Good Enough	41
Just Beyond Your Mind	128
Lend the World Your Helping Hand	125
Let's Not Wait Till Tomorrow	76
Liberate Your Mind	20
Live Kiirtan	45
Love is All There Is/Baba Nam Kevalam	60
Love is the Best	27
Love is the Best	58
Make it One With You	98
Make Me Humble	34
Mantra Kiirtan 2011	86
My Heart Will Go on Loving You	25
Nayan Majhare	134
No More Blood, No More Tears	36
Now I See You	32
One Fine Day I'm gonna go with a smile	14
Open My Heart	26
Precious Kind of Love	31
Promised Land	70
Rainbow of Humanity	13

Remember the Sun Will Shine	74
Sakal Maner Viina	131
Shower of Grace	67
Waiting for That Time	68
Sitting in the Lap of Creation	79
Spiritual Oasis	66
Squeaky Clean	94
Stay With Me Endlessly	109
Thank You	40
The Eency Weency Spider	52
The Light of Truth	89
The Lion Sleeps Tonight	80
The One True Love	100
The Secret of it All	64
The Secret of It All	95
The Wise Ones Say (written by Dada Veda)	50
The Wise Ones Say	15
This Little Light of Mine (public domain)	51
Till I Found You	7
Tiny Green Island P.R. Sarkar	57
Trickle on Down	62
We Are All Brothers and Sisters Anonymous	54
You Can Make the Sun Shine (written by Singh Kaur)	55
We are Never Alone or Helpless	122
We are Never Alone or Helpless	18
We Don't Need No Billionaires	106
We Don't Need No Corporations, Do We?	110
We've Just Got to Hang On	144
What's it Going to Be?	140
Why Should I Worry	44
You've Got to Move On	113

www.ingramcontent.com/pod-product-compliance
Lightning Source LLC
Chambersburg PA
CBHW051409070526
44584CB00023B/3357